SEMANTICS OF
NEW TESTAMENT GREEK

THE SOCIETY OF BIBLICAL LITERATURE
SEMEIA STUDIES
Dan O. Via, Jr., Editor
William A. Beardslee, Associate Editor

THE SWORD OF HIS MOUTH: FORCEFUL AND
IMAGINATIVE LANGUAGE IN SYNOPTIC SAYINGS
by Robert C. Tannehill

JESUS AS PRECURSOR
by Robert W. Funk

STUDIES IN THE STRUCTURE OF HEBREW NARRATIVE
by Robert C. Culley

STRUCTURAL ANALYSIS OF NARRATIVE
by Jean Calloud, translated by Daniel Patte

BIBLICAL STRUCTURALISM: METHOD AND
SUBJECTIVITY IN THE STUDY OF ANCIENT TEXTS
by Robert M. Polzin

STORY, SIGN, AND SELF: PHENOMENOLOGY AND
STRUCTURALISM AS LITERARY CRITICAL METHODS
by Robert Detweiler

CHRISTOLOGY BEYOND DOGMA: MATTHEW'S CHRIST
IN PROCESS HERMENEUTIC
by Russell Pregeant

ENCOUNTER WITH THE TEXT: FORM AND HISTORY IN
THE HEBREW BIBLE
edited by Martin J. Buss

FINDING IS THE FIRST ACT: TROVE FOLKTALES
AND JESUS' TREASURE PARABLE
by John Dominic Crossan

THE BIBLICAL MOSAIC: CHANGING PERSPECTIVES
edited by Robert M. Polzin and Eugene Rothman

SEMANTICS OF
NEW TESTAMENT GREEK

by

J. P. Louw

FORTRESS PRESS
Philadelphia, Pennsylvania

SCHOLARS PRESS
Chico, California

Library of Congress Cataloging in Publication Data

Louw, J. P.
    Semantics of New Testament Greek.

    (Semeia studies)
    Bibliography: p.
    1. Greek language, Biblical—Semantics.
I. Title. II. Series.
PA875.L6 1982   487'.4   81-67308
ISBN 0-8006-1511-5   AACR2

9031I81   Printed in the United States of America   1-1511

Contents

Preface

This book was first drafted in Afrikaans in 1973 as a hand-out to students in order to provide a practical handbook to the various modern linguistic theories—trying to make these insights useful as a semantic explication of the grammar and style of New Testament Greek.

Eventually, in 1976, a first edition was published in Afrikaans in which the basic theory behind this approach to New Testament Greek involved the conviction that semantics is concerned with much more than merely the "meaning" of words and phrases, as has been the case in most traditional approaches to the Greek of the New Testament, especially in New Testament grammars and commentaries. This conviction impelled me towards a theory in which the paragraph was considered to be the basic unit of semantic analysis. Word and sentence analyses are by no means discarded, but their significance is restricted by their being part of the paragraph which is understood as the basic unit of communication. Therefore, semantic analysis of New Testament Greek is, in fact, an analysis of discourse since the paragraph is the fundamental unit for the explication of discourse. Sentences are the basic units for linguistic analysis of paragraphs while words are seen as the elements by which sentences are constructed. This implies a procedure diametrically opposite to the "word-bound" methods of earlier studies in semantics of New Testament Greek. This point of view naturally has many implications for biblical scholarship.

In contrast to the "word-bound" methods, however, the order in which the material in this book is presented moves from word to sentence to paragraph for pedagogical reasons, since by this order the motivation for a paragraph approach towards discourse seemed to be best accomplished. In this way the fallacies of traditional approaches to New Testament Greek, progressing from the form of a word to its "meaning," often by means of etymology, can be exposed.

Semantics, as treated in this book accounts for the contention that meaning operates on different levels: that of words, sentences, paragraphs, even that of the total discourse. A proper understanding of the Greek text of the New Testament, essential to all exegetical studies in biblical scholarship, cannot be achieved unless the information deduced from all these levels are integrated in the reading and explication of the text.

The present English edition of this book, written during the 1977–1978 academic year and sent to the publisher in its final form in 1980, is a completely revised version of the original edition. A book comes off the press inevitably at a stage when one would want to treat various points somewhat differently, enlarge on numerous implications, etc. It is hoped, however, that the material here presented may be of some help to New Testament scholars at a time when general linguistics has advanced considerably while New Testament Greek scholarship is just beginning to "catch up" with these developments.

It is extremely important that the reader not view this book as presenting a text theory or a theory of discourse analysis. This is perhaps only a small part of such a venture, in fact, a starting point devised to analyse the semantic content of a language segment into its constituent units in order to read the Greek New Testament in a more rewarding way—with attention to important semantic features of language.

Writing a book involves a debt to one's teachers, colleagues and students as well as to the authors of numerous publications one has read through the years. To these scholars this book is gratefully dedicated.

J. P. Louw
November, 1981

Abbreviations

BAG
: *A Greek-English Lexicon of the New Testament and Other Early Christian Literature,* translated and adapted by William F. Arndt and F. Wilbur Gingrich from Walter Bauer's *Griechisch-Deutsches Wörterbuch zu den Schriften des Neuen Testatements und die Ubrigen urchristlichen Literatur,* second edition revised and augmented by F. Wilbur Gingrich and Frederick W. Danker. Chicago: University of Chicago Press, 1979.

GNB
: Good News Bible

JB
: Jerusalem Bible

KJV
: King James Version

LSJ
: *A Greek-English Lexicon* compiled by Henry George Liddell and Robert Scott, revised and augmented by Henry Stuart Jones with the assistance of Roderick McKenzie. Oxford: Clarendon Press, 1940.

LXX
: Septuagint

NEB
: New English Bible

N T
: New Testament

RSV
: Revised Standard Version

TEV
: Today's English Version

UBSGNT
: United Bible Societies' *Greek New Testament,* 3rd ed.

Chapter 1

Semantics—A New Field of Study

Semantics is concerned with meaning, and meaning must be one of the basic interests when dealing with any linguistic utterance. However, the study of the structure of meaning is a relatively new field. It is true that the ancient Greeks already speculated about the meanings of words. For example, Plato's *Cratylus* dealt with the question: does the sound pattern of an utterance inherently convey meaning or is it merely a matter of convention? Yet, for centuries afterwards little more than this was considered. A popular field of study which resulted from such an approach concerned the nature of the history of words—in particular the question of where words came from. The "real" or "true" meaning of a word was usually established by means of an examination into its history within the language. This was done in such a way that the oldest meaning was considered to be the "true" meaning. This method (discussed in chapter 4 below) was so popular that for ages afterwards it lived on unquestioned. Semantics, until recently, was never systematically examined within the study of language. This was certainly true in the case of ancient Greek, but even more so in the case of NT Greek. As yet there is no book on NT Greek that considers semantics, and the subject is not even incorporated into a section of any one grammar. This also holds true, to a large extent, in all the other fields of Greek language study. Although the large standard grammar of Schwyzer and Debrunner includes a section on stylistics, which has itself only been considered by a few other writers, not a word is found on the matter of semantics (1939, 1950).

The reason for this attitude lies in the once popular view that semantics should be restricted to the compiling of dictionaries. Consequently semantics has been concerned only with the meanings of words rather than with the *structure* of meaning. Dictionaries only treated the meanings of isolated single words with perhaps sporadic reference to idiomatic expressions or, in large dictionaries, examples of usage. This approach tended to present the most popular translation equivalents with no specification as to how far they cover the same range of meaning as the original word. For example, if we look up κύων and find that the dictionary mentions 'dog', then we have not found the *meaning*, but only a term that *translates* κύων. In Rev 22:15 κύνες does not indicate a quadruped domestic animal, but is used figuratively to signify bad people. In our culture such a description is not uncommon; consequently we probably would not notice anything strange when dogs are mentioned in Rev 22:15 along with magicians, immoral people, murderers, and the like. However, in a culture where the term 'dog' is never used figuratively it will be difficult to understand why the poor dog was classified with wicked people. On the other hand, there are languages which do employ a figurative extension of 'dog' in which it is admirable to call someone a dog. In such a language 'dog' would indicate that a person is loyal and of noble character. If someone from this language group should look up κύων, and find that it "means" 'dog', he would not understand Rev 22:15 at all. Furthermore, many dictionaries quote the "meanings" 'judgement' and 'punishment' for κρίμα. Yet, κρίμα never *means* punishment in Greek. It signifies an intellectual decision (i.e., judgement) and not an action of interpersonal requittal (i.e., punishment). But κρίμα is often correctly *translated* as punishment, as in Gal 5:10 "the man who is upsetting you . . . will be punished by God" (*TEV*). In this context the *punishment* is the implication of the *judgement*. This is indeed what the author meant by κρίμα. What is involved may be clarified by the following example: 'the police arrested the man who shot the farmer'. In this context the word 'shot' may imply that the man killed the farmer, since from the wider context this may be a logical conclusion. Yet, the term 'shot' does not in itself mean "shot dead" (or "killed"). The term 'shoot' essentially means "to cause a weapon to discharge a missile." Likewise in Gal 5:10 the κρίμα (i.e., 'judgment') of God implies that God's judgment in such cases will naturally involve a decision to punish people who do the things dealt with in the context of Gal 5:10. To render κρίμα by 'punishment' is an implication restricted to the context of Gal 5:10, and is not a new meaning of κρίμα, since Greek usage offers no example of κρίμα used absolutely in the sense of punishment. If 'punishment' is a possible translation the contexts always involve bad behavior which, if judged, naturally implies punishment.

Though the semantics of grammatical forms such as the cases, moods, genders, and so on are touched upon in the syntactic discussions of different grammars, little progress has been made beyond a treatment of each item individually. The result has been that semantic structure as such has received little attention. Weinreich claimed (1968:143) that even in recent years the bulk of work done on semantics was strongly inclined towards, as he puts it, "the semiotic process of naming in isolation." Semantics in fact, is concerned with far more than merely the meanings of words; this will be seen in chapter 10 of this study. Indeed, semantics extends over sentence boundaries and in this way it is something very new indeed.

It is striking that books concerned with the history of the study of language have treated the study of semantics only lightly. The main concerns have been a few remarks about the ancient Greeks, the Middle Ages, and an assortment of modern psychological and sociological studies dealing (mainly from a historical point of view) with the change in the meanings of words. The first complete book specifically concerned with semantics was published in 1897, and was the work of M. Bréal. Called *Essai de Semantique*, this book stood firmly in the tradition of the study of the historical evolution of words. It paid special attention to finding out *why* the meanings of words change during the course of time. Prior to Bréal semantics had been rarely mentioned, and since Bréal little more was achieved during the first half of the twentieth century.

Until about twenty-five years ago it would have been unusual to find any study concerning semantics in a linguistic publication. However, roughly a quarter of such publications today are concerned with the subject of semantics in one way or another. Moreover, at present semantics is developing into one of the basic components of linguistic study. Sörensen (1970: 67) put it as follows: "If there is such a thing as THE basic notion in linguistics, it is the notion of meaning." Chafe (1970: 73) has said that "semantic structure is the crucial component of language." This point of view has recently been confirmed more and more. Nida (1975a: 9) states: "the most intriguing aspect of language is meaning, but we have only begun to explore the intricacies of its structures and its relations to communication." Semantics is indeed a new field to be exploited, and by it we are brought to the very heart of the nature of language.

Chapter 2

Semantics—Not Only a
Linguistic Concern

In 1971 the volume *Semantics: An Interdisciplinary Reader in Philosophy, Linguistics and Psychology* by Danny D. Steinberg and Leon A. Jakobovits was published. The three fields of study mentioned in the title are certainly among the most important fields concerned with semantics; however, semantics is also of particular importance in anthropology. Let us begin then with the last of these.

ANTHROPOLOGY AND SEMANTICS

In the field of *cognitive anthropology*, where the comparison of the organization and recognition of material phenomena for a people of some culture is central—and so by implication the relation between language and thought in human customs and practices—it is often claimed that semantic structure can be correlated to the contents of culture. Language is such a part of culture that one reflects the other. The importance of this is seen in the fact that a technical periodical concerned with this field of study has the specific title *Anthropological Linguistics*. Hoijer (1953: 554–573) reviewed the work that had been done. An example of what is important in studies of this kind is the question why French, for instance, employs *tu* and *vous* in contrast to English that uses only 'you'. That is to say, why is a distinction made in one culture between intimate and polite forms of address, and not so in another? These problems are considered to be culturally important—and rightly so. However, it should not be concluded that the English are less polite than the French. Color terms are particularly interesting

5

in this respect: 'grey' and 'brown' are represented by *one* word in Navaho; the same is true of 'blue' and 'green'. This does not mean that the Navaho cannot make a distinction between these colors. Eskimo has many words for different types of snow surfaces, yet no word for 'snow' in general. In English we distinguish between 'dew', 'fog', 'ice' and 'snow', but the Koyas of South India do not. Numerous examples of this kind can be found.

Nida (1954) has described how the meaning of an action in different cultures can vary to such an extent that the same expression can have opposite meanings. The utterance 'there is a knock on the door' indicates for us that someone, usually of good intention, wants to converse with the occupants. For the Zanaki of Tanzania only thieves knock on the door to find out if anyone is at home. The words of Jesus in Rev 3:20 "Listen, I stand at the door and knock" will, for them, have to be expressed in a different way. The Kpelle of Liberia find it strange that branches were spread on the road (Matt 21:8) when Jesus entered Jerusalem. For them to put anything in another's way is an insult. They would rather sweep the road as a token of honor. Facts such as these make translating difficult, but they should not be taken to suggest that there are some deficiencies within these cultures. *It is merely a case of different meanings.* It is, therefore, of the utmost importance in semantic studies, to have a knowledge of such differences and to observe them thoroughly.

Quite another matter is the following: Whorf (1941, 1956) advanced the idea that the pattern of a language must influence behavior. He contended that a person's conception of items like time, space, matter, and so forth is bound to the structure of his language. A problem confronting this theory is that closely related languages can belong to divergent cultures, that is, Afrikaans and Dutch, or Hebrew and Arabic. Another objection is that modes of expression in languages do not necessarily illustrate characteristics of the different cultures. Indeed, the relationship can be very slight, if at all relevant. For example: Siertsema (1969) pointed out the fallacy of asserting that because an Englishman speaks of the 'foot of the mountain' he sees the mountain as a living creature in an upright stance, and therefore implies that the European is zealous, hard-working, and "always on his feet." In contrast, the Yoruba of Nigeria call the lower part of a mountain the 'seat of the mountain', and are therefore a people who are lazy and like to sit and slumber. This kind of totally indefensible reasoning is elaborated in Boman (1954). He typifies the Greek as *static* because he likes to contemplate, whereas the Hebrew is *dynamic* because he is a man of action. This contention is based on the fact that the Greek language has many abstract nouns while Hebrew has but a few. Knight (1953:8) held that "the Hebrew, almost invariably, thought in terms of the concrete. There are few abstract nouns in the Hebrew language. Even the adjective is at a rudimentary stage of development in classical Hebrew." The same reasoning was given by Friedrich (1959). These scholars, and their followers, extracted various attitudes of mind—such as those mentioned above—from phenomena which they assumed were basic to the languages involved, and then used these "habits of mind" as principles by which documents might be interpreted. Thus, as a further example, Robinson (1952) observed that Greek has two words, σάρξ and σῶμα, that can be translated for the Hebrew word בשׂר. Robinson then concluded that the Hebrew mind does not have the same capacity for making distinctions as the Greek, and consequently the Hebrew could not think in terms of 'body' and at the same time 'flesh'. Robinson finally maintained that the Pauline use of σάρξ and σῶμα is to be understood only in the light of these assumptions.

The error in this reasoning is that languages generally have one word that can be used to speak of different things while speakers *are well aware* of the differences. For example, 'tongue' in English can be translated as *tong* or *taal* in Afrikaans, yet English-speaking people have no difficulty in distinguishing between 'tongue' (= *tong*) as a body part and 'tongue' (= *taal*) as a code of communication through speech (= language). It would be absolutely absurd to conclude that the English regard language as a capacity of the tongue (= body part) only, and not of the total vocal system. What is more: the matter of "one or more words" between languages can go either way. This is the case with Afrikaans *bekeer* and the English 'repent' and 'convert', or the Afrikaans *broer* and *broeder* and the English 'brother'. What matters is not the *number* of words, but how they are *used*. In the past this was overlooked so that *words* and *thoughts* were correlated with each other. James Barr (1961:8–20) showed how this false correlation originated with Herder (1833), who was criticized for this by the linguist Edward Sapir (1907:109–42). Yet, it has lived on in popular form. Barr also refers to Knight's book (1953), where this incorrect idea was used to argue that Hebrew has few abstract nouns; consequently the concept of the Trinity was a very difficult one to grasp by the people of the OT since they could only "think concretely." Siertsema (1969) has shown how this idea of "concrete thinking" caused one theologian to assert that Hebrew had no word for the Dutch *eeuwigheid* (= 'eternity') because, according to him, they were a people of action who could not think abstractly. For him, the Hebrew word עוֹלָם was proof, for it literally, he said, means only 'a long time'. Siertsema then observed that if the Dutch word *eeuwigheid* was analyzed by him in the same way as the Hebrew, then he would find to his bewilderment that *eeuwigheid* (= *eeuw-ig-heid*) means nothing more than 'a hundred years' (*eeuw,* 'century'). The Dutch, therefore, would be even less able to think abstractly! Though it may be said that עוֹלָם does mean 'a long time' this is not the full picture. It is a generic word for a long time of variable length, and in some contexts the length is unlimited, that is, uninterruptedly continuing, everlasting. It may, therefore, very well be used to signify eternity since 'uninterrupted time' is a basic component of עוֹלָם in OT usage and is no more, or no less, abstract than our term 'eternity'.

Another example of incorrect semantics based on anthropological considerations can be taken from the article "Faithfulness and Faith" in which A. G. Herbert asserted (1955:373–9) that there is a basic difference between faithfulness in Hebrew and in the European languages (including Greek). The European languages see it as an action of man; the Hebrew as a firm quality of God. This, for Herbert, is part of the Hebrew concept of the world. The reader will observe that this is the opposite of what Boman and his supporters claimed. Greek is now taken to be the language of action while Boman attributed this characteristic to Hebrew. This is the risk we run when we take up meaning on a nonlinguistic basis: every example is explained to suit the situation.

In the case of "remote" languages, such as Biblical Greek or Hebrew, we are more easily led astray in our conclusions, most of which would never be admitted in the case of modern languages. Take the English expression 'pay a visit'. Is it ever explained in terms of a monetary payment? Is it part of the English culture to see a visit to a friend as something people *pay*? Could one maintain that such an idiomatic expression has ontological significance? How do you 'run' a risk? Asked differently: does any English-speaking person think of *running* if he hears the utterance 'you run a risk in doing that'? Yet, this is done to the languages of antiquity.

Siertsema (1969) pertinently shows that an expression such as 'the seed of Abraham' is often explained, quite unjustifiably, with the rejection of the meaning 'the descendent of Abraham'. Here, it is claimed, the original word ostensibly meant 'seed' and one would be disregarding the cultural concept in translating it as 'descendents'. In John 8:33 (σπέρμα 'Αβραάμ) such reasoning would only be valid if σπέρμα in Greek *never* meant 'descendent' but only 'seed', and that the author purposefully used it in a unique metaphorical sense.

Though the previous paragraphs *illustrated* certain pitfalls in relating linguistic items to anthropological phenomena, a knowledge of anthropology is of the utmost importance for semantics, and vice versa. At the beginning of this section on semantics and anthropology a few remarks were made to this effect. It remains to enlarge on the proper relationship between anthropology and semantics. However, the question of how far cultural metaphors are relevant to semantic interpretation is a difficult feature in the process of explication. As yet little has been done apart from showing what is wrong. On the positive side, an open field of research lies ahead in determining reliable methods and procedures. In Eastern cultures the dragon is not a threatening beast, symbolic of evil powers. In the East it is a symbol of good luck and prosperity. What then, of the translation of δράκων in Revelation? Or, what of the 'white garment' of a holy person in the Korean language, since to them white is a symbol of mourning and sorrow, not of purity. In some cultures it is a strange thing that the publican "beat his breast" when he prayed. To 'beat your breast' is a Biblical idiom of regret, a confession that the person acted wrongly. In other cultures it is a token of pride and self-satisfaction. Take the difficult case of αἷμα in the NT with reference to the redeeming death of Christ on the cross. T. H. Brown (1968:8), in a review of the *TEV* translation said that the *TEV* translation of Acts 20:28 negated the cultural coherence of the OT's "shedding of blood" as a vehicle of reconciliation by translating "which God made his own through the death of his own Son." Brown insisted that one *must* translate "with his own blood" and not "through his death." However, the *TEV* translation is a precise rendering of the *meaning* because διὰ τοῦ αἵματος does not merely mean 'blood' as a liquid of the body. If that were the case, then it would have been unnecessary for Christ to die on a cross. He could, with respect, have cut a vein to let some blood. Clearly, blood was a symbol of death! As a matter of fact, the OT usage of blood as a symbol of reconciliation was not simply concerned with blood, but blood was the token of the death that paid for sin. The victim had to die. Indeed, the punishment for sin was death. The reader, not having the symbolism of the OT beforehand, will not deduce this fact from "blood." That is why the *TEV* translation is a good one because it is concerned with meaning. The cultural context should rather be indicated in a footnote. Yet the anthropological significance of blood is semantically well represented by rendering αἷμα as 'death'. In such a way 'death' is a figurative extension of the meaning of αἷμα.

An important criterion concerning this matter is that adjustments *can* be made on the basis of anthropological significance, except in the case when the cultural picture would be completely distorted. If, for example, we alter the person "possessed by an evil spirit" to one who has "a nervous problem," we totally depart from the Bible's doctrine of the existence of evil spirits. The message of the original text would then be totally misinterpreted. This has a parallel in one of the modern trends among some European theologians to replace the word 'God' in the Bible with 'Reality'; and this is done with an appeal to semantics—an appeal that is misplaced because modern semantics not only considers single words, but also the meaning of the entire context. This means that we must never make cultural adjustments without acknowledging the total communication. Adjustments should only be made if they aid the communication of this totality. An example is the *NEB*, which is perfectly correct in translating γύναι in John 2:4 as 'mother', and not 'woman'. It is a cultural adjustment which makes the meaning more explicit. However, an adjustment such as 'I just got a brain wave' for the literal 'thus says the Lord' is totally misplaced, because the original is quite clear in its literal form. The adjustment would not transfer the meaning because it brings a new meaning in conflict with the message of the original. To find the efficient cultural equivalent is difficult. Therefore, it is necessary not to start with the single word or expression, but rather to consider these at the end since semantics goes beyond word boundaries. This is a basic principle of semantics which will be discussed in chapter 10. A final example of a proper cultural adjustment may suffice. D. J. Clark showed (1976: 214) how a translator in Bangladesh employed anthropological data to find a suitable semantic equivalent in his language for the Greek of Eph 2:20 ἐποικοδομηθέντες ἐπὶ τῷ θεμελίῳ τῶν ἀποστόλων καὶ προφητῶν ὄντος ἀκρογωνιαίου αὐτοῦ Χριστοῦ Ἰησοῦ. The problem was how to translate θεμελίῳ ('foundation') and ἀκρογωνιαίου ('cornerstone'). In Bangladesh people have bamboo and thatch buildings. They do not dig foundations or use stones. For 'cornerstone' Clark and his friend considered 'corner poles'. This cultural adjustment was then tested against its significance in the wider context of Eph 2:20, as well as in NT times. The cornerstone carried the diagnostic component of 'the most important stone' in the NT world, yet the corner poles in Bangladesh were not the most important ones in a building. Finally they decided that 'foundation' in Eph 2:20 was equivalent in cultural significance to 'roof ridgepoles' in Bangladesh, while 'cornerstone' was equivalent to the 'central upright pole'. This made the meaning of Eph 2:20 perfectly clear to the readers in Bangladesh in the same kind of picture as Paul used for his original readers.

PSYCHOLOGY AND SEMANTICS

Steinberg (1971), in reviewing the latest contributions of psychology to semantics, showed that it is only recently that growing interest in the interrelationship of these two fields has focused attention on the role of *meaning* in the function of the process of learning. Steinberg (1975) emphasized the fact that psychologists have contributed relatively little to the understanding of semantics. Yet, the problem of *how* a speaker is able to communicate information through the use of sentences is a fundamental psychological and semantic problem. The stimulus and response functions that words and their associations have in relation to human behavior have gradually become an important concern in psychology.

On the other hand, linguists have become interested in an amalgamation of the concerns of linguistics and psychology within an area labeled "psychosemantics." Chafe (1973) showed how people generally would understand an utterance such as 'Mr Wilson broke his arm' as referring to the immediate past, though the utterance itself contained no specific reference to the immediate past. Nida (1975d) pointed out some serious mistakes made by translators as a result of inadequate understanding of the relations between language and psychological processes. A proper understanding of these relations will help to appreciate how essentially the same information can be communicated in a variety of ways. Nida showed, for example, how one language may have a preference for passive constructions, and another for active ones. What is important in such cases is not the formal structure, but the meaning which is carried by such forms. This contention implies that passives in one language need not necessarily be rendered by passives in another language. Nida also indicated how some have insisted that the Gospel of John must make a distinction between two kinds of love, since in John 21:15–17 two different verbs, φιλέω and ἀγαπάω, are employed. Yet, a careful investigation in terms of the total discourse of the Johannine writing reveals a marked preference on the part of John to substitute closely related terms. Though ἀγαπάω and φιλέω *can* differ in meaning in other contexts, it is apparent in John that the two terms are used in conjunction merely for stylistic effect.

In the area of semantics, psychology largely combines language and behavior, especially with reference to how humans react to certain language utterances. This is very important in translation. A literal translation very often arouses incorrect reactions, and consequently an incorrect understanding of the original utterance. The importance of this fact cannot be overestimated in exegesis. For example, in the RSV the words of Jesus in John 2:4 τί ἐμοὶ καὶ σοί, γύναι are rendered "O woman, what have you to do with me?" The "O" gives an [unnecessarily?] solemn tone to the reply, while the rest arouses amazement because it sounds ill-mannered to address one's mother in such a way. The New Berkeley Version is little different: "Woman, what right do you have to tell Me?" The American Standard Bible is downright harsh and impolite: "Woman, what do I have to do with you?" The psychological impact of the ASB suggests a stronger rejection than the other two translations—at least to the present writer! The intention of the Greek, which is very different, is only seen when taken in the broader context, and when realizing that a highly idiomatic phrase—in fact, a Semitic idiom—is employed. At the wedding there is a shortage of wine, and Jesus' mother tells him: "Their wine is finished." Jesus' answer consists of two conjoined idioms: τί ἐμοὶ καὶ σοί and οὔπω ἥκει ἡ ὥρα μου. The first idiom indicates a reaction of amazement by the hearer, that is: 'why do you tell me?' or 'what has it got to do with me?' Jesus is not the Master of Ceremonies, so why should the supply of wine be discussed with him? The second idiom means that there is no reason for haste: the speaker will give attention to the matter in a short while. Jesus' psychological reaction to his mother's statement about the wine is fully motivated. Yet, his further remark showing that he is not offended since he is, nevertheless, willing to pay attention to it, evoked Mary's reaction to the servants: "Do whatever he tells you to do!" The total context shows that both Jesus and Mary understand each other in a benign way. The psychological impact of τί ἐμοὶ καὶ σοί could not have been harsh. The New International Version translates it as "why do you involve me?" This is much better. Perhaps we could render it more appropriately as 'Mother, you really want to involve me, don't you!'

Several of the psychological approaches to meaning have no direct value for linguistics. One example of this is the theory of the image of thought referred to by R. Brown (1958: chap. 3). Here the "basic" meaning of a word is connected to the thought image associated with the word-symbol. This has value for psychology, but seems to be of little concern for linguistics. However, some linguists have used the fact that it is an impossible task to measure all images and all stimuli to prove (?) that semantic research cannot be done systematically. This is an overstatement based on irrelevant presuppositions. For some time this point of view has hampered semantic research.

On the other hand, psychology does propose some suggestions that could be used by linguists, as was seen above in the reactions of the speaker and hearer in the process of communication. A very important insight which came from the study of meaning in psychology caused linguists to recognize certain psychological factors involved in the process of language learning and use. As a result, linguists realized the fallacy of the popular belief that people store ideas in the brain in some sort of verbal form, and that language is, therefore, basically a matter of words. Early studies in semantics were, to a large extent, "word-bound." Once it was realized that a word's meaning is inevitably connected to other words, and that meaning goes far beyond word boundaries, semantics made considerable advances. This will be dealt with more fully in chapters 9 and 10.

PHILOSOPHY AND SEMANTICS

The most penetrating studies in semantics have been done in linguistics and philosophy, but since they overlap in so many areas, it is important to make a clear distinction between the approach to semantics in these two fields. In linguistics an utterance is analyzed merely to determine the semantic *content* of the utterance, without being concerned primarily with its *meaningfulness*. The latter is the concern of philosophy, especially logic. Therefore, from a linguistic viewpoint, there is nothing peculiar in the statement 'the man is a woman'. This sentence is correctly structured by the syntactic rules of English, while the semantic content of this sentence is that two persons are to be classified as identical: the first person is a male, and he is said to be a female. Semantically, from a linguistic viewpoint, it is a case of *experiencer* ('man') and *condition* ('is a woman'). It is of no concern for linguistics whether the facts are true or not, or whether they agree with the sentence statement or not. However, according to the principles of logic, the meaning of this sentence is unacceptable (or at least highly improbable) because the two components are contradictory. In formal logic, sentences such as these are usually considered out of context, or at least in a minimum-context situation. What counts is the truth value of the proposition. In linguistics, the context in which such an utterance is used is of primary importance if one has to press for the meaningfulness of the utterance. For example, suppose a situation where someone hears the name Jo Kaspers, and accepts it simply as the name of a man while the conversation partner knows that Jo Kaspers is a woman. The wrong supposition could be corrected by saying 'the man is a woman', meaning the person whom you keep on referring to as a man is indeed a woman.

This introduces a consideration of the utmost importance in language usage: a linguistic utterance is semantically determined by the situation in which it is uttered. It is also important to realize that "situation" means any background information, or the lack of it. This was shown by Ziff (1964). Without any situational information one has to depend entirely on the syntactic and morphemic structure of an utterance. In this case a statement such as 'the man is a woman' could be meaningless. In certain contexts, however, it could be properly meaningful, even logically acceptable, because the implicit information from the context allows us to understand more than merely the *word content* of the utterance. And this "more" is certainly a part of semantics.

Jerrold J. Katz (1964) has described the sentence 'the man bit the dog' as a semi-sentence. Linguistically it is a well-formed sentence, but logically poses a somewhat unusual situation—yet, one that is not impossible. Therefore, to designate such sentences as semi-sentences means to impress logical judgements on language. A sentence such as 'scientists truth the universe' is also called by Katz a semi-sentence, because 'truth' is a noun used strangely within the word string 'scientists . . . the universe'. A verb is demanded to complete the sentence. This judgment is, again, a logical one based on the presumption that the language symbol 'truth' can only be a noun. Yet, it is part of the flexibility of language that the term 'truth' can be used by means of a linguistic transformation as 'make true, show to be true'. Compare a similar example, 'to bible a hotel' meaning 'to place bibles in a hotel'. McCawley (1968) rightfully rejected this kind of idea as proposed by Katz. He quoted sentences such as 'he says that he smells itchy', 'he says that he poured his mother into an inkwell', 'John said that the rock had diabetes', and claimed that "there is nothing anomalous about reporting that someone has said something anomalous." Katz finally conceded (1965:160–161).

It is important to distinguish logical judgments from linguistic ones, and for this reason Saumjan (1970) used the terms "linguistic semantics" and "logical semantics." Coseriu and Geckeler (1974: 103) used similar terms, "linguistic semantics" and "semantics of logicians." The term 'semantics' is, therefore, used differently in philosophy and linguistics respectively. One must pay attention to this fact when reading the literature, and one has to judge contributions accordingly. For example, Carnap's "Foundations of Logic and Mathematics—A Logical Analysis of Language" (1964) can be clearly seen from the title to be concerned with logic. The same applies to Evans and McDowell, who edited a collection of essays under the title *Truth and Meaning: Essays in Semantics* (1976). However, Wells's article "Meaning and Use" (1954) does not state (in its title) whether linguistics or logic is the concern. These few examples, taken at random, show clearly that care must be taken when working with the literature on semantics, and one must not assume without question that a work has a linguistic purpose simply because "meaning" or "semantics" is used in the title.

However, it is important not to separate logical semantics from linguistic semantics. J. M. E. Moravcsik (1974:3–35) has shown the interdependence of these two fields in the study of meaning. The study of meaning by anthropologists and psychologists has made valuable contributions to linguistics—and the same is true for philosophers. Logic is important when dealing in a given context with little background information in distinguishing between the different fields of meaning of a word. The so-called incompatibility of utterances is also of importance here. McCawley (1968) says that 'my aunt is a bachelor' can only mean that my aunt is a graduate, if treated logically in a minimum context. The sentence 'her red hat is blue' might be "correct" if her red hat had fallen into blue paint.

The relationship between semantics and logic is treated clearly by J. W. Oller (1972). He showed how the famous sentence of Chomsky: 'colorless green ideas sleep furiously' was *not* an example of the claim that grammar is independent of meaning. This claim was made on logical considerations based on the literal meaning of the terms. Oller says that this sentence could well be understood in English as 'insipid immature ideas lie dormant in a state of potential explosiveness'. Only when the syntax is disturbed as in 'furiously sleep ideas green colorless' does it become meaningless. Oller argues rightly that syntax, semantics, and situation (his "pragmatics") are related to each other.

The material discussed in this chapter should indicate how semantics is a field of study having several dimensions: linguistic, logical, psychological, anthropological. This may be the reason why it is such a complicated and controversial field of study. All these dimensions must be distinguished from one another without separating them. This fact will be taken into account in the following chapters. Finally, linguistics must be the dominating dimension with the others supporting it, since language is a linguistic entity in the first place.

Chapter 3

Semantics—An Area of Contention

The impossibility of measuring every thought image and stimulus was mentioned in chapter 2. This fact strengthened the belief, held by many linguists some decades ago, that semantics could not be studied in a systematic fashion. It was especially noted by some philosophers that it was doubtful if one could understand meaning without a nonlinguistic experience of the subject matter. Jakobson (1959) referred to Bertrand Russell, who said that a person can never understand the word 'cheese' if he does not make contact with the real thing (cheese) in a nonlinguistic situation. Jakobson correctly revealed this reasoning to be false. How would it be possible to understand abstract ideas, or study ancient languages, if Russell were correct? This kind of reasoning by Russell negates the phenomenon of association. Nyíri (1971) claimed that this view of meaning is based on an incorrect conception of what meaning really is, namely that the meaning of something is thought of either as an aspect of experience, or as a thought image—thus objectivizing meaning. Wells (1954) also claimed that Russell's definition has a persuasive basis that is, however, false, since meaning would then have to be the relation between object and token. Such a view, claimed Wells, returns to the problem of Plato's *Cratylus* (see the beginning of chapter 1).

Leonard Bloomfield provoked this kind of reasoning in one of the most influential works in linguistics, *Language* (1933). Bloomfield's dominance in linguistics at that time was one of the main reasons why there has long been an aloofness by linguists towards semantics. In chapter 9 of *Language,* Bloomfield reasoned that one must have a thorough scientific knowledge of something to know its meaning, yet because human knowledge is not comprehensive, meaning cannot possibly be studied. He used 'salt' as an example and argued that the scientific way to describe it is 'sodium chloride', but words like 'love', 'hate', and so forth have no such scientific terminology. The majority of words cannot be explained in the same way as 'salt', and so Bloomfield had to keep semantics out of linguistics. However, Bloomfield's contention is incorrect since the term 'sodium chloride' still does not give any palpable experience of what it refers to. It is only another term which defines 'salt' within the confines of chemistry. And if one gives a paraphrase of 'love', one has already begun an attempt to define it. After all, one does not have to know *everything* about an item in order to say *something* about it. If Bloomfield were correct, all language usage between people would be senseless, yet it is known from experience that people do understand each other—and it does not matter that this understanding is not always complete. Oller (1972: 45) showed how Chomsky (1957) continued with the same idea as Bloomfield, and how this was opposed by several writers who likewise contended that the real use of language by people, as observed daily, would be totally inexplicable if this view were maintained. Chomsky later modified his view (1965).

One of the basic problems concerning the disputes about semantics is the problem of the continual usage of the term *meaning* without saying what is meant by it. This matter will be discussed in chapter 8, but for the sake of a better perspective a few aspects of the problem will be touched on here. C. C. Fries (1954) gave the following definitions: (a) the meaning of a sentence is that which a speaker wants the listener to understand. In other words, meaning is understanding. This seems to be satisfactory, but—as will be shown later—meaning and understanding appear to be different things; (b) meaning is everything one can infer; (c) it is the relation between ideas; (d) it is the expectation aroused, and so on. These kinds of definitions are vague enough to be useless, yet they illustrate how "easy" it was thought to define meaning.

It is outside the scope of this study to explore the meaning of the term 'meaning' in English, and yet one must give an account of the use of the word 'meaning' in this particular context. The contribution made by Sörensen (1970) gives a valuable insight into this problem.

Sörensen maintained that one finds oneself in a vicious circle when defining 'meaning' as "meaning is the meaning of meaning." To get out of this dilemma one should first say what meaning is *not*: (a) Meaning is not the *denotatum* of a thing. That is, it is not the thing pointed to. Sörensen does not give an example, but one can illustrate it as follows: 'he is ill', and 'the man is my brother' may have the same denotation, say, Peter. Yet 'he' and 'man' in these two sentences do not have the same meaning. Therefore meaning is not the same as reference. This also implies that *words* are not *things*. We can speak of a person's will, reason, mind, soul, and the like without necessarily referring to separate entities, as is the case in Matt 22:37 ἀγαπήσεις κύριον τὸν θεόν σου ἐν ὅλῃ τῇ καρδίᾳ σου καὶ ἐν ὅλῃ τῇ ψυχῇ σου καὶ ἐν ὅλῃ τῇ διανοίᾳ σου. In this particular context the terms καρδία, ψυχή, and διανοία do not refer to separate identifiable entities. They are employed as a unit to signify the total human being. If not, man should be said to consist of only three aspects, or else the command enjoins to love God only with specific parts of the personality. Sörensen continued his argument in saying that one must understand *meaning* and *denotatum* in the following way: identity of meaning entails identity of denotatum; identity of denotatum does not entail identity of meaning.

(b) Meaning is not the *idea* of something. When arguing that 'square' is the 'idea' of a square, or the 'square-idea', or the 'idea of the notion of a square', one must *first* have the idea of the notion in order to identify it with the square. Then we have the idea of the idea of a square, but to have this, we must have the idea, of the idea, of the idea of a square *ad infinitum*. By this argument Sörensen emphasized the basic linguistic fact that we cannot attach meaning to words, but rather only words to meaning. This feature of meaning will be returned to later on.

(c) Meaning is not the *knowledge* of denotata. One cannot say 'child' means everything man knows about children. (This is especially valid with regard to the positions of Russell, Bloomfield, and the others discussed at the beginning of this chapter.) The knowledge of children is not a knowledge of the language *term* 'children'.

What is meaning when stated positively? Sörensen said: "a meaning is that which makes a sound a linguistic sound, in general; that without which nothing is a linguistic entity; and it is that which determines what is denoted by the sign of which it is the meaning." To illustrate the significance of this definition, Sörensen continued:

A statement like " 'dad' means male parent and is used by children and has the effects resulting from this usage" is just nonsense, whereas " 'dad' means 'male parent' and is used by children and has the effects resulting from this usage" is not. That is to say, the word 'dad' MEANS 'male parent' and IS (but does not MEAN) used by children, and HAS the effects consequent upon this usage, but does not MEAN them.

What Sörensen's contention means can be illustrated by the following example. When someone says: "I will know what the graphic sign ὕδωρ means if I can define ὕδωρ" he really has not given any answer, because ὕδωρ still is a token for that definition. In other words, the meaning of ὕδωρ is a token (in the form of a definition such as H₂O) with the same meaning as ὕδωρ. What we have determined, in reality, by this reasoning is that the two tokens have the same meaning. If we argue: "I will know what the token ὕδωρ means if I know the conditions something must satisfy to be called ὕδωρ," then—according to Sörensen—this is an explanation of what it is to know the meaning of ὕδωρ. This apparently ingenious reasoning allows one to realize that it is not a matter of the meaning of a word that is important, but rather a matter of the word used for the meaning. That is to say, the starting point is *meaning* and not *word* because one wants to arrive at a definition of **meaning**. Sörensen, therefore, maintains that meaning is the condition something must satisfy in order to be indicated by a word, or words. His account is logical, yet it contains the kernel of a notion which is basic to linguistics: meaning is not so much something associated with words, but rather words are tokens to be associated with meanings. This means that a language does not first find a particular word and then look for a meaning to be associated with that word. On the contrary, words are only symbols or tokens to signify an entity. Sörensen correctly concluded that "to introduce a new sign is not to introduce a new meaning." For example, the phonological token represented graphically by the token 'proton' in English, does not first exist, and is then given a meaning. Rather the thing which is 'a positively-charged unit in the composition of an atom' first exists, and then the term 'proton' is used to signify it as a "shorthand" graphic token.

The fallacy of working from word to meaning was the reason for the incorrect idea that meaning in a language, that is semantics, cannot be systematically examined. It also gave rise to the extremely dangerous fallacy that meaning is found *within* a word, and to understand this "inner" meaning one, consequently, has to find the origin of the word since the meaning of a word is derived from an assumed basic meaning (the so-called *Grundbedeutung*). This gave rise to the etymological method which will be discussed in chapter 4.

A further consequence of the above-mentioned belief is that a word really has only *one* meaning, even if there are different usages of it. In translation, therefore, a word has to be constantly rendered by one particular gloss if the translation is to be really "faithful." This astonishing view has gained many followers, and will be discussed in chapter 6.

Finally, the insight that it is incorrect to begin with *words* in a semantic analysis, emphasized how semantics is concerned with more than merely the "meaning" of words. Meaning is what one intends to convey, and words are but one item employed in this process as symbols representing particular features (in fact, a set of relations) of that meaning. This is the basis of all modern semantics and will be discussed in chapters 9 and 10.

Chapter 4

Etymology

Investigations into semantics have often been limited to single topics within the history of linguistics in which only certain aspects of language were considered. One of the most popular views in this field can be dated back to the ancient Greeks. It concerned the conviction that a word *has* a meaning, and debated the question whether there was any direct relation between a word and its meaning. This has since become part of *tradition*. Nida (1975a:14) showed that:

> The meaning of verbal symbols has traditionally been regarded as some kind of attribute or inherent property belonging to words. In large measure this opinion may be due to such expressions as "the word has this meaning . . ." or "this word's meaning is . . . ." But meaning is not a possession, it is a set of relations for which a verbal symbol is a sign.

Though linguists generally maintain that the *traditional* view expressed above is misleading, and in fact erroneous, the legacy of centuries seems to hold its ground, not only among people in general, but also among scholars engaged in various hermeneutic activities. Even today, we occasionally find opinions related to Plato's *Cratylus,* one of the oldest documents (380–70 B.C.) concerned with semantic problems. In the *Cratylus* we have a discussion between Socrates and two young men, Cratylus and Hermogenes, who defended their viewpoints from opposite directions. The problem at issue was whether the meaning of a word is found in its nature (φύσις) or whether it is a matter of convention (νόμος or θέσις). In practice this is to ask why the Greek word for 'run' is τρέχω. Is it because of

23

something in the sounds τ + ρ + ε + χ + ω which suggests running? In the *Cratylus* it was attributed to the letter ρ because of its fast movement or vehemence (the Greek *r* is not the same as the English, but more like the Scottish). This is then applied to words such as τρόμος ('tremble, shake'), ῥοή ('streaming, flow'), θραύω ('break into pieces'), and so on.

It should be noted that the idea of fast movement and vehemence lies in the *meaning* of words such as these and was transferred from this to the letter ρ since there are many words without a ρ that have this same aspect of meaning, that is, θοάζω ('run, move fast'), πτόα ('fear, trembling'), νᾶμα ('streaming'), ἄγνυμι ('break into pieces'), and the like. Moreover, there are many words with ρ that do not have any feature associated with fast movement or vehemence, for example, τράπεζα ('table'), ῥόδον ('rose'), and στρῶμα ('mattress'). This dispute was senseless, but it maintained its appeal through the centuries—probably stimulated by Socrates' decision to accept Cratylus's viewpoint (φύσις) as the only possible way to arrive at the (assumed) original process of naming which took the characteristics of things into consideration. Socrates accepted this starting point of Cratylus instead of the simpler approach of looking first at the language as a whole rather than just a few comfortable examples.

In the controversy whether words originated φύσει or νόμῳ, the Stoics also chose the side of φύσις. Through their powerful influence on the thought of the time, the idea of ἔτυμον (or 'real meaning') became deeply rooted in the understanding of language. When the *form* of a word would not readily lead to its 'meaning', it was believed that one should go back far enough in the word's history to find the 'real meaning'. This pursuit was called ἐτυμολογία, hence etymology—a quest originally concerned with proper names, yet soon extended towards finding the 'deeper' meaning of any word.

The ancient Greeks extended this approach by explaining grammatically related words with one another: Ζεύς was declared overlord because its accusative form Δία was said to indicate that everything was made by (διά) him. Even names in other languages were explained by Greek words. The name of the Egyptian god Osiris was explained as ὅσιος ἱερός, 'holy consecrated'. If this method were correct, then everyone would need to know Greek in order to understand the true meanings of words.

This conviction, that the key to a word's meaning lies somewhere in its form, was held through the centuries and was the most important element in the belief that the true meaning of a word could be derived from its etymology. In other words, if we know the origin of a word, then we can understand and determine its true (ἔτυμος) meaning (λόγος). In Plato's *Cratylus* we encounter various examples such as ἄνθρωπος meaning 'man' because it is derived from ἀναθρῶν ἅ ὄπωπεν 'look up to what he saw'. The Stoics explained θάλασσα ('sea') in the same way as θανάτου ἆσσον οὖσα 'that which is nearer to death'. The word κνώσσειν ('sleep') was explained as κενοῦν τοῦ ὄσσειν 'empty of looking'. In later times such phrases were readily developed as, for example, the well-known explanation of the Latin word for 'window', *fenestra,* as *quae nos ferens extra* 'that which leads us to the outside'. This kind of reasoning is certainly of the utmost folly, yet illustrates the point arrived at from the idea that the meaning of a word can be determined from its φύσις. On the other hand, this kind of reasoning for centuries conditioned the way in which people thought about the relation between a word and its meaning.

However, it is obvious that a word at the time of its origin *can* be closely related to some occurrence or situation. Yet, in most cases it is impossible to track it down; and even if one is fortunate to establish the circumstances, it has generally been the case that as a word was rapidly established, its original meaning was lost. Siertsema drew attention to this point in a study of the Yoruba of Nigeria. These people were inoculated for the first time in 1956, and they designated the process as *ko nomba* because it appeared to them that *a number was carved* on the people. At first the Yoruba connected this meaning with the process, but soon *ko nomba* became the conventional term for inoculation. Later the Yoruba were amused to learn of the word's origin.

At present one of the basic principles of semantics is that the relation between the form of a word and its meaning is an arbitrary one. The Afrikaans word *groente* ('vegetables') does not make us think of *groen* ('green'). Beans are green and the leaves of vegetables are mostly green, but the majority of vegetables are not green. Even if we would stress the point that the word *groente* originated from an association with 'green', this does not say anything today. Moreover, *groente* probably originated from *groei* ('grow') etymologically. Yet *groei* is of no help in understanding *groente* in Afrikaans. Etymology merely tells us where a word came from and how it developed. Etymology is concerned with the history of a word, not its meaning in a specific context.

A very interesting example of the attempt to derive meaning from etymology in modern literature can be seen in Barclay's commentary on Paul's letters to the Corinthians (1975). He explained the meaning of ὑπηρέτης in 1 Cor 4:1 as basically designating 'a rower'. This 'meaning' is based on etymology deriving ὑπηρέτης from ἐρέσσω 'to row'—a derivation which has become extremely popular in NT writings. Probably R. C. Trench (1854) was one of the main agents in promoting this kind of etymology. Trench wrote under the entry ὑπηρέτης that "he was originally the rower (from ἐρέσσω)." However, the term ὑπηρέτης never had this meaning in classical Greek. It was a term generally used for a servant, an attendant. The etymology of ὑπηρέτης was derived from its morphology, namely ὑπό + ἐρέτης. The term ἐρέτης occurs in Homer for a 'rower'. Therefore, J. B. Hofmann (1950) explained ὑπηρέτης (for which he gave the general meaning 'servant') as meaning basically 'assistant rower' or 'subordinate rower'. The same is found in Robertson (1931:102) without even commenting on how ὑπηρέτης came to mean 'under-rower', since in all other passages in the NT it merely signifies a servant. It is noteworthy that Trench did not use the notion of 'assisting' or 'subordination' as part of his fuller definition running as follows: "ὑπηρέτης was originally the rower, as distinguished from the soldier, on a war-galley." Barclay went a little further by designating the ὑπηρέτης as "a rower on the lower bank of a trireme." Morris in the *Tyndale Series* (1958) designated the ὑπηρέτης as "a servant of a lowly kind." This shows how an etymological explanation acquired additional features by association with the rowers of a trireme, and Morris even adds a specific status feature which, in the context of 1 Cor 4:1, would give a special turn to the exegesis of the passage. C. K. Barrett is right (in *Harper's NT Commentaries*) in remarking that ὑπηρέτης in 1 Cor 4:1 is little different from διάκονος since in NT usage hardly any distinction of meaning can be made between these two terms when referring to servants. Some scholars, however, refer to an inscription from the island of Cos reading τοὶ ὑπηρέται τᾶν μακρᾶν ναῶν ('the attendants on the large vessels'), taken to refer to rowers, yet this inscription dates from the *first* century B.C., and the meaning 'rowers' is probably taken from the assumed etymology. Therefore LSJ rightly designated this meaning as dubious.

To determine the "original" meaning of a word from its constituent parts, that is, explaining ὑπηρέτης as from ὑπό + ἐρέτης, can lead to serious misunderstandings. In word compounds the constituent parts are often not related to the whole expression. In English a 'butterfly' cannot be associated with 'butter' + 'fly'. If so, one would have to assume a totally different basic meaning for other language groups; for example, Afrikaans for butterfly is *skoenlapper* which would then have to be analyzed as *skoen* 'shoe', and *lap* 'rag'. Barr rightly calls such an analysis a "root fallacy," and Conklin (1967) mentions the following examples for English: "a *poison oak* is not an oak tree that is poisonous; a *pineapple* is not an apple, nor even less is it from a pine tree; a *grandson* is not an elegant boy. Likewise there is no fountain in a *fountainpen;* an *earring* is very often not a ring; *strawberries* are not made of straw, etc." To determine the meaning of a word from its form is extremely misleading. Even if one thinks that the fountain of a fountainpen is a suitable association, it must be remembered that when the word was first coined to indicate a kind of pen, the focus was on the fact that such a pen did not need to be frequently dipped into ink. People initially could have associated the idea of a fountain with this kind of pen, but soon it became a standard form and people were only aware of this association after being told about it.

Compounds in NT Greek can tempt us to fall into the same problem when we seek an etymology based upon morphological elements. In this way ἀπόστολος is usually explained directly from its morphology as one who is sent out, from ἀπό + στέλλω. Though 'send out' could be thought of as *one* aspect of ἀπόστολος, it is in no way the focal point. The entire article on "Apostle" in Pop (1964) is based on the notion that everything that can be said about ἀπόστολος centers on the concept of 'the one sent'. This is again based on the untenable assumption that the form of a word must be directly related to its meaning—and consequently the focus of a word is neglected! The word ἀπόστολος is semantically nearer to ἄγγελος 'messenger' than to ἀποστέλλω 'send out'. Hastings's *Dictionary of the Bible* puts it correctly as "the proper meaning of ἀπόστολος is an ambassador, who not only carries a message like an ἄγγελος, but also represents the sender." In other words 'a special messenger, a representative' is closer to the meaning of ἀπόστολος than 'one sent out'. 'Special messenger' provides the focal point while 'one sent out' acts as an implicational element in the background. As such 'one sent out' may have a role, but definitely not the dominant one. The basic principle involved is that of the progression from meaning to form; not from form to meaning. That is to say, from the meaning 'special messenger' we can progress to ἀπόστολος as the term used to signify this meaning, but we cannot "analyze" the constituent parts of ἀπόστο-λος and think that the sum total of the data provides the *meaning* of ἀπόστολος.

On the other hand, one should not entertain the idea that compounds *cannot* have the meanings of their different parts. Sometimes this is true if the meaning coincides with the sum of the meanings of the parts of the word, but one can only recognize that it is so through the meaning which must be known beforehand. In this way ἐπιτίθημι means 'add' in Rev 22:18. One can then say that meaning and form are correlated *in this example,* ἐπί + τίθημι = 'place' + 'with' = 'add (to)'. In Acts 13:4 ἐκπέμπω *means* 'send out', and ἐκ + πέμπω is justified as 'being out' + 'send'. But in the case of παρακαλέω it would be misleading to explain its meaning as παρά + καλέω = 'to your side' + 'to call', and then to continue explaining the "real meaning" as 'to call to your side'. In NT usage παρακαλέω belongs to three semantic domains which can be represented by (a) 'request, beg', (b) 'encourage, urge', (c) 'comfort, cheer up'. To see 'to call to your side' in each is absurd. Furthermore, the noun that is related to παρακαλέω morphologically, παράκλητος, is not 'one called to another's side' in the NT. It should also not be linked up with either (a), (b), or (c) above—and certainly not signifying the comforter (that is [c] above), as is usually thought. In NT usage the focus of the word is on 'one who helps'. In translations such as Moffat, Goodspeed, Williams, and the *TEV* it is rightly translated by 'helper'. Though it may be possible in certain contexts, to think of a helper as one who is called to one's side, the meaning 'helper' has a far broader range than merely 'call to one's side' which may, in itself, be one small facet of the meaning 'helper'. Therefore, 'call to one's side' is not the point of focus.

It is a basic principle of modern semantic theory that we cannot progress from the form of a word to its meaning. Form and meaning are not directly correlated. Just as we cannot explain the English term 'understand' as meaning 'under' + 'stand', so we cannot explain διαχειρίζω in Acts 5:30 as 'to lay hands upon vehemently'. The word only means 'to kill'. How it was done is a matter of context, not lexicography. So also in Matt 24:51 διχοτομέω should not be explained as δίχα ('in two') plus τέμνω ('cut') since the word simply means 'punish severely'.

A striking example of this is found in the article by Daube (1950), where he challenged the translation of συγχράομαι in John 4:9, "Jews do not mingle with Samaritans." He pleaded for the meaning followed by Hendriksen (1953) and Barrett (1978) in their commentaries on John; a meaning also followed by the translators of the *NEB*, namely 'the Jews do not use vessels together with the Samaritans'. Barrett even said (p. 232): "it should rather be rendered according to its etymology." On this interpretation συγχράομαι, taken as σύν + χράομαι, is said to reflect a Rabbinical regulation that labels the Samaritan's daughters as constantly impure "from the cradle onwards." Hall (1971) responded to Daube in an excellent article showing how the Rabbinical regulation is surely an illustration of the Jewish attitude towards the Samaritans, but it definitely is not indicated by συγχράομαι. The word itself takes the dative object apart from the σύν which was emphasized so much by Daube. Hall is justified in concluding "that the natural meaning of συγχράομαι is not 'to use along with others', but 'to make use of'. . . ." The word appears with objects as 'make use of', or with persons as figuratively meaning 'to mingle with, associate with'. Daube and his associates overlooked the fact that they want to force the meaning of συγχράομαι when used with objects onto John 4:9, while all the time the context was clearly concerned with people. Moreover, in this forcing they have to 'import' the word *vessel* to justify the meaning. How *vessel* is derived from the etymology is never said.

The "real" meaning of ἁμαρτάνω ('sin') in the NT is often explained in terms of its oldest usage as found in the epics of Homer, more than eight centuries before the NT. In Homer ἁμαρτάνω regularly occurs in situations referring to the missing of a target, such as to discharge a missile vainly, to miss one's aim, to miss a person in throwing something to be caught, etc. This is then taken over as the 'hidden meaning' of ἁμαρτάνω in the NT, generally used for the meaning 'to sin'. Sin, therefore, 'really' means to miss the purpose (target) God put us on earth for. This kind of etymological analysis had the consequence of making plausible such an explanation, but in no way can 'to miss the purpose' be considered the *real* meaning of ἁμαρτάνω in the NT. It cannot be used as the yardstick to judge whether something should be regarded as a sin, or not. In order to know what sin is we must consider the *passages* in the NT (in fact in the whole Bible) that deal with sin, not a particular *word* used to signify sin. The meaning of 'sin' is therefore extracted from the sentences and paragraphs that deal with sin.

On the other hand it is important to study all the words and phrases *used* for 'sin'. This is done to determine first, whether there is a generic term for sin; second, whether some terms bring into focus certain specific aspects of sin (*not* the 'hidden meaning'); third, whether certain writers had a preference for particular terms; and fourth, whether some terms had emotional overtones, and so on. In the case of ἁμαρτάνω, this term will be discovered to be the most generic for 'sin'. It may cover the whole semantic field, while a word such as ὑπερβαίνω has its focus only on the breaking of a commandment as a feature of sin. Likewise παρακοή focuses on disobedience, that is, to refuse to listen to; παραβαίνω (often used along with νόμον) highlights the fact of acting contrary to established custom or law; πταίω suggests figuratively that sin involves a stumbling; ὀφείλημα emphasizes that sin involves guilt, and the like. That is to say, that these terms make explicit what is already implicit in the Biblical concept of 'sin' for which ἁμαρτάνω is the generic term.

A very important fact, always neglected when ἁμαρτάνω is explained etymologically as 'to miss a target', is that among the oldest usages of ἁμαρτάνω contexts can be found in which ἁμαρτάνω not only meant 'to miss a target', but also 'to make a mistake, to be deprived of, to lose, to neglect' (see LSJ). Why is 'to miss a target' taken as the "hidden meaning," but not one of the others? Furthermore, if etymology is to be used, why go back only as far as Homeric Greek? Why not even further to ἁ + μαρτος in which μαρτος goes back to a stem σμερ from which μέρος 'part' is derived. This derivation is given by J. B. Hofmann (1950) as the origin of ἁμαρτάνω. Thus, the basic meaning would be 'not to have a part in'—a meaning which can be easily applied to 'sin'. In fact, the concept 'sin' has so many facets that it takes little imagination to link any of the above mentioned "meanings" in some way or another to a favored explanation of the basic notion of sin.

From what has been presented in the previous pages it has been shown how the etymological method does not account for one of the most basic aspects of meaning. This is the fact that the meaning conveyed by a particular word is continuously subjected to change. There are many factors that play a part in this change. The users, for example, of a language do not use words in an absolutely consistent way. The nature of language allows them to extend the field of a word, to reduce it, or to transfer it. The causes are quite difficult to ascertain since they are concealed by many circumstances distributed over a long period of time. The Greek word ὄρνις first meant 'bird', but later it was increasingly used for the feminine bird, the 'hen'. In the NT 'hen' is the common meaning. The word ἴδιος once was a strong word for 'one's very own', but by NT times it was weakened and often occurs as a synonum for αὐτοῦ. The reasons for this can no longer be discovered. The fact, however, remains that it is decisive for any semantic study to know whether the older meaning still exists at the later stage.

Chapter 5

The "General" Meaning
of a Word

Etymology does not provide an original meaning that acts as the basis for every other meaning of a word. So, how can it be explained that one can very often "feel" that there is something that binds together the various meanings of a word? Is there no global idea that joins together these meanings? Take for example γένος. Dictionaries have the following "meanings": 'race', 'descendent', 'family', 'nation', 'kind', 'species'. Can it not be argued that the idea of a relationship binds them all together? In other words, are these meanings not all specific, or specialized, applications of the idea of relationship? Furthermore, can it not be argued that the most general meaning of γένος is in fact 'relationship'? To answer these questions two observations must be noted: (a) 'Family' could just as easily be the most general, or global, meaning if we would replace 'family' by 'relationship' in the list above. So, how do we determine which is the most general? (b) What is actually at stake is not a general meaning, but a common component. That is to say, 'relationship' is not a general meaning but a common component, and as such does not say anything about the focal features of each of the separate meanings in the list above. Therefore, what is often regarded, or sensed, as something binding meanings together, is not a "general" meaning, but a *common component*. Real insight into the various meanings of γένος comes from the focal features represented by these components of meaning that distinguish the meanings from one another.

However, "general" can be considered from another perspective. Within all the possible meanings, is there not one that is *used* the most?

This meaning can easily be called the most "general" meaning. So, if the different meanings of a word are examined, and it is found that meaning (a) is valid for 80 percent of the occurrences while (b), (c), and (d) are valid for only 10 percent, 7 percent, and 3 percent, respectively, then it can be argued that meaning (a) is the most general as far as frequency of usage is concerned. The others would then be secondary meanings. The idea of a secondary meaning is problematic since it easily leads to the idea of a meaning that is subordinate. The term "general" (occasionally also called "central," or "normal," or even "natural") is useful only as long as it is never raised to the status of implying that it is the root or basis of meaning. This "general" meaning must always be understood simply as the most common in frequency of occurrence. And for that matter it may also be called the common meaning.

This sense of "general," or "common," meaning is close to what linguists would call the unmarked meaning. *Unmarked* is understood as that meaning which would be readily applied in a minimum context where there is little or nothing to help the receptor in determining the meaning. Consider the example of the sentence 'he does not want pumpkins'. If it is heard without any other background information available, then most English-speaking people will probably understand that he does not want a certain kind of vegetable. That is to say, their first reaction is to classify 'pumpkin' as a vegetable. It may very well be so because pumpkin is commonly used to signify a type of vegetable. This meaning is the unmarked meaning. Reading the sentence as 'he does not want stupid people' will only arise where the reference to people is known from the context, or if the sentence has a reference to a person as in 'he is a pumpkin', since this figurative meaning always applies to people. The general meaning of 'pumpkin' in English is a kind of vegetable and is the meaning *most* people will think of first when the word is heard. It is important to note that this is a matter of frequency, not meaning. Often the meaning that one first hears, or encounters daily, will be the one that is most "natural," or "normal," or "general" to that individual. Wonderly (1968:109) stated that if the context is unclear, then different people will understand a specific utterance differently, since this is seen to be determined by their individual background and experience. A sentence such as 'they had a large amount of stock' can be understood as referring to cattle by people with a farming background. To the stockbroker the term 'stock' normally signifies shares in a corporation, but to the merchant it will indicate his inventory of goods. This does not mean that these people will not be aware of all the meanings signified by the term 'stock'. It is merely a matter of which meaning is central to their experience. This meaning will then be to them the *unmarked* meaning. As soon as there is some restrictive element, such as 'die' in the sentence 'a lot of their stock died', the intended meaning is interpreted alike by people whether they are farmers, stockbrokers, or merchants. Such restrictions exclude other interpretations—either totally, or partially, as in 'he owns a lot of stock in that company'. This sentence will exclude the possibility of reference to animals, though 'inventory' will not be totally impossible. In doubtful cases the broader context usually will settle the matter except in cases of real ambiguity. This is because words signify only *one* meaning in each specific context in which they are used, except for rare instances where a speaker *purposely* intends a play on meanings. But even if *two* meanings are purposely intended in a context, it merely shows that the author wants his receptors to acknowledge *two* readings of a particular sentence. This is often the case in poetry. Yet, in each reading the said term will signify only *one* meaning. Therefore, to maintain a common kernel as the general meaning among all the possible meanings that may serve as a factor behind all the other meanings, and which serves as a type of 'inner' meaning, is absurd. In the case of 'fox' signifying a cunning, sly person, one may argue that this is a figurative extension of meaning related to the animal, a fox. Thus 'animal' may be the common denominator! Such an argument is missing the point that though 'fox' in a sentence such as 'he is a fox' can be related to the meaning 'a wild quadruped of a particular kind', it is a figurative extension involving a totally new meaning. This relationship between 'wild animal' and 'cunning person' is secondary. It cannot serve as a general, or central, feature since the focal features in 'wild animal' and 'cunning person' have nothing in common. The meaning 'cunning' semantically links with 'sly, subtle, crafty, wily, stealthy, astute, artful, underhanded', etc. That is to say, there is a much more prominent relationship between 'cunning' and these terms, than between 'cunning' and 'fox'. This raises an important linguistic point which can be illustrated by the following example on a wider basis: the term τράπεζα occurs in the NT in contexts such as (a) τὰς τραπέζας ἀνέτρεψεν "he overturned their tables" John 2:15, (b) παρέθηκεν τράπεζαν "he served them a meal" Acts 16:34, (c) ἔδωκας τὸ ἀργύριον ἐπὶ τράπεζαν "you put money in the bank" Luke 19:23. To look for a unifying general meaning behind these three occurrences such as taking 'table' to be "central," from which 'meal' can be derived by relating it to a table used to eat at, and to derive 'bank' from a table used by money changers to place money on, may be interesting encyclopedic information concerning the history of the term τράπεζα and its usages. Yet, such a common feature does not define the actual *meanings* involved; it rather shows how it came to pass that the same *word form* acquired the possibility of being able to serve as a term for the different meanings.

This type of approach has led L. Goppelt (in *TDNT*, Vol. VIII) to discuss the term τράπεζα under the headings "General Use" (including its etymology τετρα + πεζα = 'four' + 'foot'), "Dining Table," "Moneychanger's Table," and "Table for the Show-Bread." The idiom διακονεῖν τραπέζαις (Acts 6:2) signifying commercial activities related to the conduct and transaction of money matters, i.e., 'to handle finances', is discussed under the "Theological Table Sayings" as a feature of "The Table of Table Fellowship" and is thus explained as referring to the "common sacral meals of the primitive community in Jerusalem."

However, the semantic significance of τράπεζα in examples (a), (b), and (c) above is not arrived at by looking for a common denominator which can serve as a general meaning, but it is determined by the distinctive semantic fields designated by the features of meaning involved in each case. Thus, τράπεζα in example (a) relates to various kinds of artifacts, especially furniture. The specific context of John 2:15 shows that the reference there is to the tables *used* by money-changers. Whether these tables were *used* to eat at, or to place money on, or to serve some other purpose, does not alter the meaning of τράπεζα. It still signifies 'a table'. The *context* defines its usage. Therefore, example (c) above, is not properly defined by relating it to the tables used by money-changers, since in Luke 19:23 the focus is not on tables being involved, but on an establishment for safeguarding money and related exchanging of monetary items. It thus involves commercial activities, not an item of furniture. As such the usage of τράπεζα in John 2:15 and Luke 19:23 relates to quite different semantic domains. Likewise, example (b) above belongs to yet another semantic domain, namely that of physiological processes involving eating, and as such signifies a unit of eating, that is 'a meal'. There is much more in common semantically between τράπεζα in Acts 16:34 and δοχή ('an elaborate meal', Luke 14:13), or ἄριστον ('a noon meal', Luke 14:12), or ἀγάπη ('a fellowship meal', Jude 12), or δεῖπνον ('the principle meal of the day', John 13:2) than between τράπεζα in John 2:15 and Luke 19:23 above. Likewise the idiom διακονεῖν τραπέζαις 'handle finances' in Acts 6:2 has much more in common with τράπεζα 'bank' in Luke 19:23 than with τράπεζα 'table' in John 2:15.

The focus of a word is highlighted by the semantic fields, and not by the (historic) relations between usages employing the same word form. If these relations are sought for, then *polysemy*, which is one of the basic semantic notions found in all languages, cannot be appreciated. Polysemy (discussed in chapter 6) states that a particular form of a word can belong to different fields of meaning. There may be an historic relationship, but this has hardly any semantic significance.

Therefore, if one has to search for a common or general meaning that combines all the meanings for which a word is used, then the item found will in no way be the basic kernel, but rather a secondary or subordinate entity. In this way ἡμέρα will mean 'day' in most cases in the NT, but in 1 Cor 4:3 it means 'law court'. This is a rare meaning, yet it is unnecessary to recover the idea of 'day' in the meaning 'law court'. The possibility that this meaning developed from 'day' is of no importance since 'law court' is a new and different meaning having its own essential features.

Chapter 6

One Word, One Meaning?

The old view that a particular word must, as far as possible, be translated by a particular gloss which is regarded as its proper meaning is closely related to what was discussed in the previous chapter. One of the most famous examples in the NT is δικαιοσύνη which is nearly always translated as 'righteousness'. Another is σάρξ, that is generally translated as 'flesh', or πνεῦμα as 'Spirit/spirit'. The essential idea is that 'righteousness', 'flesh', 'spirit' are seen as the basic meanings. The "secondary derivative" meanings are only used when the first does not fit the context. If it does fit, even in the most unnatural way, then it is still retained in most instances. Matt 24:22 reads ". . . no flesh be saved" (i.e., 'nobody be saved'), John 1:14 "the Word was made flesh" (for 'the Word became a human being'), Rom 9:8 "children of the flesh" (instead of 'children of natural birth'), Heb 5:7 "days of his flesh" (for 'during his earthly life'), Rom 8:12 "to live according to the flesh" (instead of 'to live according to human nature'), Jude 7 "to go after strange flesh" (i.e., 'to practice sexual immorality'). In all these divergent cases σάρξ is translated by 'flesh', and this reveals the conviction that 'flesh' is the central meaning of σάρξ. Even worse is the assumption that 'flesh' adequately expresses these divergent meanings in English—which, of course, is not the case. It is, therefore, unwise to ask what the meaning of 'flesh' is in the NT, and by this question to suppose that there is *one* word in Greek which always means 'flesh'. Furthermore, it is often assumed that there is something 'mysterious' behind this word, something to be known if the 'real' meaning of σάρξ 'flesh' is revealed. On the contrary, one can never say what σάρξ means, but only what it means in this or that context. From all these contexts a picture of the different possibilities of meaning signified by σάρξ can be built up. And even then one still does not have *the meaning*, but only the possibilities of meaning. In a specific context, however, one can justifiably say that σάρξ means this or that. To always award one meaning to one word is incorrect since it denies the basic fact of polysemy. Polysemy is a matter of the economic utilization of forms. A language would be quite unwieldy if it had a separate word for everything in existence. To overcome this problem different things are denoted by the same form. In Greek the form μέρος signifies a 'part' or 'piece' of something, or it denotes a region as a 'place' or 'district'. It is also used to reproduce the meaning of 'trade' or 'business', to name a 'party', or 'sect', to denote the 'side' or 'edge' of an object. The verb ἐξέρχομαι can signify to 'go out', or 'come out, disappear, descend from'; εἰμί can be used for 'is, exist, happen, come, go, stay', etc. The word ληστής designates a 'robber', but also a 'rebel'; παῖς a 'son', or 'daughter', or 'slave'. It requires no skill to multiply similar examples, for dictionaries are full of them. Linguistically, it is incorrect to say that παῖς means 'son', rather we should say 'son' is one of the items that could be designated by using the word παῖς, i.e., that παῖς *can* mean 'son'.

It is important to note that when a word is used outside a context, we can say that the word (or rather, that the sound pattern or character) is a language symbol by which different things could be indicated, and then a list of such things could be given. More specifically this implies that a word does not have a meaning without a context, it only has possibilities of meaning. When used in a context, the situation and the syntactic environment contribute to the choice between the several possibilities of meaning. The word has a specific meaning in that context. This implies that a word does not have many possible meanings in a particular context. If contexts are identical then a word can be consistently translated by the same word. Although a word has only one meaning each time it is used, there are exceptions, to which attention has been drawn in the previous chapter. This has been shown to occur in the case of intentional ambiguities. At this stage, an example may be supplied to illustrate the point: in John 1:5 Bible translations and commentaries differ between the two meanings 'overwhelm' or 'understand'. Both these meanings are possible for καταλαμβάνω, and both fit the context of John 1:5. We have to say either that the author had only one in mind, which one is hard to say; or we have to conclude that the author intended both meanings by a play on words. But even then the two meanings are not mixed, for if the context is understood in a specific way the word signifies only one specific meaning. "Overwhelm" renders a feeling of joy—the darkness did not overwhelm the light; "understand" renders a plaintive tone—the darkness did not understand the light. Such a play on words often occurs in John. It is characteristic of his style. In the context of John 1:5 he saw the confrontation between light and darkness from two perspectives: triumph and melancholy. It does *not* mean that 'overwhelm' and 'understand' must be mixed, and so result in a claim that the action of overwhelming includes a kind of understanding, or vice versa. If this were done we would be performing an "illegitimate totality transfer" according to Barr (1961).

In Rom 15:27 the word λειτουργῆσαι appears in a context concerned with financial help to the congregation in Jerusalem. In this context the word only means 'to help'. The *NEB* translates ἐν τοῖς σαρκικοῖς λειτουργῆσαι appropriately by "to contribute to their material needs." The *JB* reads "to help them with temporal possessions"; the *TEV* "to serve the Jews with their material blessings." Another possible meaning for λειτουργῆσαι in Koiné Greek is 'to serve religiously', as in Acts 13:2 and Heb 10:11. The latter context refers to priestly service. The noun λειτουργός means an 'official', or a 'servant', or a 'priest' (Rom 13:6, 15:16). Each one is a meaning of its own, and must not be mixed. Vincent (1887) made the error of an "illegitimate totality transfer" in claiming the priestly idea in Rom 15:27. He argued: "by using the word for priestly service, Paul puts the ministry of almsgiving on the footing of a sacrificial service. It expresses the worship of giving." Vincent assumed that 'priestly service' is the central idea in the word in each context it is found. Why this is so is never explained. A. T. Robinson (1951) is correct: "it has no sacerdotal functions in 15:27."

Such a totality transfer is often extended by putting Hebrew and Greek words together. It is probably done unthinkingly under the impression that because the OT and NT form one Bible, the Hebrew and Greek languages can also be joined together. A good example is given by Barr (1961:187–188) where he criticized T. F. Torrance

(1956/7). Torrance argued that because the Hebrew אֱמֶת is translated by ἀλήθεια, πίστις, and δικαιοσύνη in the LXX, it must be grasped that "where in the New Testament we have ἀλήθεια we must understand that not simply as a Greek word, but in the light of the Biblical inclusion of πίστις and δικαιοσύνη in the concept of truth." Torrance consequently maintained, on the ground of the OT Hebrew, that ἀλήθεια in the NT means "the reality of God in covenant relationship, God's being true to himself, truth as grounded upon God's faithfulness." But can this be true in Mark 5:33, where it is said about the woman who touched Jesus' garment that she told him the whole truth upon being questioned who it was who touched him?

The erroneous consequence of a "totality transfer" can also be illustrated in modern languages. In the sentence 'the hall was taxed to capacity', the term taxed means only 'filled' or 'occupied'. Only *this* meaning is relevant. The other meanings of 'taxed' such as 'demand', 'accuse', 'assess', not even to mention 'taxation', are not relevant at all. There is no point in reasoning that the idea which covers and binds these meanings together is 'to burden'—and that the hall was then burdened with people. This explanation is *not* what is thought of in everyday English when the sentence is heard. What is understood is merely that the hall was filled to the brim.

Chapter 7

Words Only Partially Overlap Between Languages

The consistent translation of one word by a specific word in a different language is at variance with another basic linguistic idea, namely, that words only partially overlap between languages. If correlative words in different languages were completely equivalent semantically, translation would be a very simple mechanical process. Complete equivalence is never the case between words in different languages, and this also suggests that a word only has a meaning in a specific context, since different languages would use different words in different contexts to render the same meaning. Compare, for example, the translations that were given for σάρξ in chapter 6 (cf. our observations on pp. 39–40).

There is, however, a deeper level at which words in different languages do not overlap in meaning—and this deeper level is not always easily discerned. When the translation 'house' is given for αὐλή in a dictionary, one must not accept without question that everything understood by the English term 'house' is also understood for αὐλή. It can be asked whether αὐλή is a large or small house, or a private house, or an official residence? Moreover, αὐλή is never used to indicate the household, that is the people, as in a sentence such as 'my house and I will serve the Lord'. When questions such as these are considered, it is soon discovered that dictionaries are in the main concerned with translation equivalents rather than meanings. In semantics the concern should be with meaning rather than words, for words only partially overlap between languages. Graphically this can be represented as:

The same principle is also valid for the synonyms of a given language. Synonyms are *not* words having the same meaning, but words that *may* have the same meaning; that is to say, they overlap in certain contexts. In Greek ἀγαπάω and φιλέω are synonyms that could be graphically compared as:

This means that there are cases in which the words ἀγαπάω and φιλέω are certainly equivalent to each other, and therefore interchangeable. There are, on the other hand, cases when they differ from each other. Synonymous words in the same language and translation equivalents between different languages thus show areas of overlapping as well as areas of difference. Words can be identical in meaning in some contexts, or more accurately, they can be symbols for the same meaning, and in other contexts they stand apart. Words such as these are only partially interchangeable. In Scottish 'this' may be used with singular or plural, while English distinguishes between 'this' and 'these'. The English 'this' is therefore different from the Scottish 'this'. The English 'that' is distinguished from 'this', 'these', and 'those', but 'that' in Scottish can cover all four English words: 'this, that, these, those'.

The examples quoted above illustrate the fact that our starting point must be *meaning* rather than *words*. A semantic analysis must, therefore, begin with the related meanings of different words rather than with the different meanings of the same word. This means that linguistically it is important that we must analyze meanings and the words signifying them rather than words and the meanings they have. Though we generally, in everyday language, speak of "the meaning(s) of a word" or of "a word having a meaning," we have already shown in the beginning of this study that meaning is not a "possession," that is, something which a word *has,* but that meaning is a set of relations for which a verbal symbol is a sign, a point strongly advocated by Nida (1975a:14). Therefore, when someone says "this word means this or that" or "this word has the meaning. . . ," what must be understood is that "this word is a token or symbol for this or that meaning." If meaning (and not the word) is our starting point, the fact that words between languages only partially overlap becomes a natural phenomenon, since each language talks about a particular meaning in its own way. Yet, all languages can talk about the same meaning, and for that matter about all meanings.

The whole argument of this study has been the contention that there is no one-to-one relationship between words and meanings; not between languages, and not even within the same language. It has been stated that one must start with meanings rather than words. Therefore it must now be explained what meaning is, what "kinds" of meaning there are, how they are to be presented, etc. It will be seen from chapter 9 onwards that semantics embraces far more than merely the so-called meaning of a word.

Chapter 8

What Is Meaning?

Definitions of 'meaning' in dictionaries describe the usage of the term 'meaning' in the particular language dealt with by the dictionary. Such definitions are therefore inadequate to define meaning as a linguistic phenomenon in semantic studies. The well-known book by Ogden and Richards (1923) is still one of the bravest attempts to define 'meaning'. Yet, 'meaning' in philosophy, psychology, anthropology, linguistics, and so on, cannot be defined in simple terms. It is a notion that has too many facets. Ullmann (1951: 6) said: "it is a commonplace since *The Meaning of Meaning,* and especially its formidable Chapter VIII: 'The Meaning of Philosophers,' that logicians, psychologists and others have so overworked that term that it has become scientifically unusable." It is noteworthy that Pei in his *Glossary of Linguistic Terminology* has omitted the term "meaning." Fodor (1977) stated in her second chapter "What is Meaning?" that "this question has been repeatedly asked, and variously answered, throughout the history of philosophy and related disciplines. Along with problems about free will, the nature of time, and so on, it has seemed one of the ultimate metaphysical puzzles."

Since *meaning* has too many facets to be adequately defined, it seems reasonable at this stage not to add any more unworkable definitions, but rather to show how different features of meaning illustrate basic principles, and from all these principles to try to understand how meaning operates in linguistic semantics. And as far as linguistic semantics is concerned Nida's statement, quoted in the previous chapter, that "meaning is a set of relations for which a verbal symbol is a sign," seems to be a workable principle if "verbal symbol" is extended to include not only single words, but also discourses.

Meaning, therefore, has to do with a multiplicity of relations by which people communicate. These relations can function on different levels, and so we have to acknowledge a variety of meanings with reference to a particular stretch of communication. Wittig (1977: 75) stressed that "different readings . . . by different readers yield different meanings," and T. R. Hofmann (1976) claimed at least eighteen different types of meaning. Though one may not accept all the distinctions he made, they nevertheless point to the many-sided nature of meaning.

What makes meaning even more difficult is that one cannot even know exactly from a text what the meaning (or intent) of the author was. Nida (1979:103) showed that:

> Emphasis upon the author's intent is generally stated in terms of what the author must have been thinking when he wrote such-and-such a word or phrase. If the author is still living, a translator may be able to consult him and try to determine just what he had in mind. But many authors are honest enough to admit that they themselves are not always sure, especially when they review articles written some years before. In fact, most highly creative persons are subject to many influences, some of which they are usually unaware; hence it is frequently quite impossible for an author to reconstruct what he had in mind or what may have influenced his thinking. It is therefore even more hazardous for the literary critic than for the translator to be dogmatic about what an author must have meant, and why he used certain expressions.

One can only analyze the text at hand and try to establish what the text says—and then hope that the text is a fair representation of the author's intent.

A. Reichling (1966) illustrated the complexity of the matter by claiming that if anyone heard the sentence 'I took the train' he may know the meaning of each word as well as the meaning of the sentence as a whole without understanding what the encoder intended to communicate. He could, for example, say that the meaning is 'I travelled by train', but this could be an erroneous interpretation of the sentence. The encoder could have used the sentence 'I took the train' to inform another how, when he was in doubt about which of two or more gifts to buy his son, he decided to buy the toy train. Thus, the meaning of the sentence on the word level may have different interpretations according to the reference of 'train', and so two different events can be meant by the sentence. To ask "what is the meaning of 'I took the train'?" is a different question from asking what is understood by the utterance in a particular situation. Meaning and understanding, or meaning and comprehension, have therefore to be distinguished from each other. Or, if we prefer to use the term *meaning* to designate that of the words, the sentence as such, and the sentence with reference to a particular context, we have to acknowledge different types of meaning. Similarly one can read the creation story in Genesis, or Shakespeare's *Hamlet* and understand all the words, and phrases, and sentences, yet without catching the intention. This type of meaning is a meaning that is not necessarily the sum of the meanings of the words, and so on.

Idioms are noteworthy in this respect. An expression such as 'to burn one's fingers' does not mean according to the meanings of the individual words. This idiom which means 'to get into trouble from meddling' has nothing to do with the event of 'burning' or objects such as 'fingers'. Idioms may best be regarded as lexical units. Their meaning has nothing to do with the meanings of the individual words constituting the idiom. Similarly Luke 9:60 ἄφες τοὺς νεκροὺς θάψαι τοὺς ἑαυτῶν νέκρους should be understood as 'you understand me wrongly; this is not what is at stake'. Mark 2:19 υἱοὶ τοῦ νυμφῶνος definitely does not mean 'the children of the bride chamber', yet this is the meaning of the separate words. The expression as a whole means 'the wedding guests'. Must it be understood that Pilate really mixed the blood of the people with their offerings in Luke 13:1 reading ὧν τὸ αἷμα Πιλᾶτος ἔμιξεν μετὰ τῶν θυσιῶν αὐτῶν? How could he have done it? Rather, it means that Pilate killed them while they were busy offering sacrifices. Furthermore, what does Paul want to say in 1 Cor 3:2 γάλα ὑμᾶς ἐπότισα? From the context it is clear that he did not give the Corinthians milk to drink. The words, on their own, cannot make us understand that Paul had elementary teaching in mind. What is the meaning of πληρώσατε τὸ μέτρον τῶν πατέρων ὑμῶν in Matt 23:32? If we render it as 'you completed what your fathers started', or 'you continue to do what they did', we have not translated the *words*. The meaning of the sentence is quite different from the meaning of the separate words.

A further aspect illustrating this problem arises from an example such as 'my bicycle broke and I do not know when I can repair it'. To say that *it* means 'bicycle' would be incorrect. Thus, if 'it' is looked up in a dictionary the meaning 'bicycle' will never be found. Yet one easily understands 'bicycle' when 'it' is used in this sentence. Just as a distinction is drawn between meaning and understanding, so must a distinction be drawn between meaning and reference. The word 'it' does not mean bicycle; it *refers* to bicycle. The hearer understands that 'it' intends 'bicycle'. The intention, and for this matter the intended meaning, is not understood from the meaning of the word, but from its reference. Yet, the lexical meaning of 'it', namely, 'object substitute' should not be discarded. Referring to one's bicycle as 'it' serves to avoid repetitiousness. One could have phrased the sentence as 'my bicycle broke and I do not know when I can repair the thing'. The term 'thing' likewise refers to bicycle, but does not mean it. The meaning of 'thing', namely, 'generic object' serves to add a note of disgust to the understanding of the intention. 'Thing' adds emotive meaning, not because 'thing' is in itself emotive, but because its co-occurrence in this sentence conveys disgust. Meaning as a set of relations involves a multiplicity of features at a variety of levels.

The distinction between meaning and reference is a basic principle of semantics. In the Book of Revelation δράκων means a 'dragon', yet refers to the devil. In 1 John 2:1 παράκλητος means 'helper', yet refers to Christ. In other contexts in the NT it refers to the Holy Spirit. Nida (1975a:15) put it as follows:

> One of the reasons for confusion as to the nature of meaning is the tendency to confuse meaning (*Bedeutung*) and reference (*Bezeichnung*). The meaning of a word consists of the set of distinctive features which makes possible certain types of reference, while reference itself is the process of designating some entity, event, etc. by a particular symbol.

Nida continued to show how two different utterances which do not *mean* the same can *refer* to the same item. An example would be 'morning star' and 'evening star', both referring to the planet Venus. In the same way 'my uncle', 'an insurance salesman', and 'a resident of Oklahoma City' all may *refer* to the same person, though each utterance is entirely different in meaning. However, although it is necessary to clearly distinguish between meaning and reference, one should not separate these altogether, since there always exists a relation between them. Meaning makes reference possible, and the frame of reference assists us in determining meaning. The term 'animal', for example, can refer to pets, game, livestock, birds, fish, dogs, elephants, etc.—and therefore can be called a generic term for a large group of living organisms. In this case it is possible to refer to many objects by the use of a single term 'animal' since all these creatures share a common feature expressed by 'animal'.

In Acts 27:17 the term βοήθεια occurs, which is sometimes translated as 'rope' or 'cable'. It can certainly be translated this way in Acts 27:17 and in similar contexts, but it must be remembered that 'rope' or 'cable' is not the *meaning* of βοήθεια. The term *means* 'help', and in Acts 27:17 it *refers* to the kind of help(s) with which a ship was reinforced in those times, probably ropes or cables. Thus in Matt 5:23 δῶρον means 'gift', but refers to a 'sacrifice'; in Luke 12:36 ἄνθρωποι means 'people', but refers to 'servants'; in John 8:32 ἀλήθεια means 'truth', but refers to 'Christ'; in Acts 6:1 διακονία means 'service', but refers to the 'distribution of funds'. The term σῴζω means 'to release someone from dangerous circumstances and to restore to safety'. In Matt 8:25 the reference is to physical circumstances when during a storm the disciples woke Jesus with the words "Lord, save us, we are sinking." It may also refer to the metaphysical and religious concept of being released from the power and guilt of sin in redemption. This is the case in Matt 1:21 where it is said of Jesus that he will save his people from sin. The question now arises why the same meaning is found in Matt 1:21 and Matt 8:25 with two different fields of reference rather than two different meanings. Would it not have been simpler to say that σῴζω *means*, (1) 'to save from physical danger', and (2) 'to save from the power of sin'? On the face of it, this seems an attractive explanation, yet it must be carefully noted that σῴζω *itself* merely means *in both* cases 'to release someone from dangerous circumstances and to restore to safety', a meaning which can easily be rendered in both cases by 'to save' in English. The 'physical dangers' and 'the power of sin' arise from the contexts. In other words, if σῴζω is taken on its own, then the kind of dangers and the nature of the circumstances are not apparent. This is an important principle of semantics, namely, that the meaning for which a word serves is only that which the word itself, on its own, contributes to the context. That is to say: what a word says of itself is the meaning for which the word is used in a specific context.

What the above argument amounts to is the important insight that meaning operates on different levels: on the levels of the word, the sentence, and the whole context. This is the reason why a distinction is often drawn between meaning and translation. In Gal 4:16 ἀληθεύω means 'to speak the truth', and belongs semantically to the field of meaning generally called communication. The *TEV* translates accordingly "have I now become your enemy by telling you the truth?" The *NEB*, however, translates it as "have I now made myself your enemy by being honest with you." In English 'to be honest' belongs to the semantic field of moral behavior, and this is not what ἀληθεύω means. However, 'to be honest' and 'to speak the truth' both amount to the same thing *in this particular context*—the former can be said to be the implication of the latter in Gal 4:16. The *TEV* translated the meaning of ἀληθεύω; the *NEB* conveyed the inferential meaning, the implication of the context. Both versions are good with regard to the task of translation, but with regard to exegesis it is clear that one has to start, not with the translation equivalent, but with the meaning based on what is implied by the context.

Meaning and implication are often confused with each other. J. Kodell held (1974) that the expression ὁ λόγος ηὔξανεν 'the word grew' means 'the numbers of the church increased'. This is the implication of ὁ λόγος ηὔξανεν, but the meaning is only that 'the message spread'. That is why the author added καὶ ἐπληθύνετο ὁ ἀριθμὸς τῶν μαθητῶν in Acts 6:7. From this the idea can be derived that the numbers increased. It is therefore wrong to speak of an 'ecclesiastical tendency of λόγος'.

The features involved in such notions as meaning and understanding, meaning and reference, meaning and implication, discussed above, show quite clearly the difference between a word's meaning and its usage in a context. Yet another area illustrating the difference between meaning and usage should be noted, namely the co-occurrence of words. Often features associated with words which are used in conjunction with other words are transferred from one to the other. In John 13:4 τίθημι is used with ἱμάτια. The *phrase* means 'to take off clothes', but such a combination can easily lead to the assumption that since τίθημι is used in John 13:4 of the taking off of clothes, τίθημι itself means 'to take off, undress'. This can then lead one to explain τίθημι in Matt 22:44 ἕως ἂν θῶ τοὺς ἐχθρούς σου ὑποκάτω τῶν ποδῶν σου "until I put your enemies under your feet" as actually meaning 'until I have clothed out your enemies', which may then be figuratively understood as 'until I have totally destroyed your enemies'. It is true that in Matt 22:44 the total idiom τίθημι ὑποκάτω τῶν ποδῶν means 'to conquer', but it is not as strong in meaning as 'totally destroy'. In both John 13:4 and Matt 22:44 τίθημι merely signifies the event of causing something to be in a place, i.e., 'to place'. When used with ἱματία the phrase indicates the taking off of clothes. This usage cannot be transformed into a meaning of τίθημι which can then be applied to other usages.

Another example can be found in BAG under πρόκειμαι. Three meanings are given: (1) 'be exposed to public view, be exhibited', Jude 7 πρόκεινται δεῖγμα "they are exhibited as an example"; (2) 'lie before, be present, be set before', Heb 12:2 ἀντὶ τῆς κροκειμένης αὐτῷ χαρᾶς "instead of the joy that was set before him," i.e., 'was within his grasp'; (3) 'of a goal or destination' 1 Clem 63:1 ὁ προκείμενος ἡμῖν σκοπός "the goal that is set before us." Semantically πρόκειμαι is an abstract signifying a locative case relation 'be at hand'. Therefore only entry (2) in BAG applies to the meaning of πρόκειμαι, while the explanation 'was within his grasp' is a legitimate implication. In Jude 7, entry (1), the meaning is merely 'they are (at hand as) an example', but the usage of πρόκειμαι in Aeschylus Septem 965 of corpses lying in state induced BAG to assume, on the basis of this usage, that 'exhibit' is a meaning of πρόκειμαι. The corpses lying in state were naturally exposed to public view, but this is an implication based on the nature of the occasion. The term πρόκειμαι in Septem 965 merely signifies that the corpses are here. The same argument applies to entry (3), since σκοπός carries the idea of goal or destination, προκείμενος means 'is at hand'. If entry (3) is not recognized as a usage, a person can easily take it to be a meaning, and then apply it to Heb 12:2 as was done in BAG. It quotes Heb 12:2 under entry (2), but also under entry (3) as a possibility, in which case it offered the translation "the joy that was in prospect for him." This shows that they did not regard entry (3) as a mere usage, but as a true meaning. One may do the same in Heb 12:1 for τρέχωμεν τὸν προκείμενον ἡμῖν ἀγῶνα "let us run the race that lies before us." It may be understood as the race which has a destination in prospect, or the race that is to be run, now and here. The possibility chosen by the exegete will surely result in a quite diverse understanding of Heb 12:1. In the one case the race will be seen as a particular kind of race, namely, the race which will bring us to the desired destination, that is the Christian race. The other explanation will want us to be engaged in the race at hand, here and now, the race of daily life. That is, to live our daily life, to be engaged in the affairs of daily life.

Meaning, and not usage, is imperative to exegesis. If usage were to be our guide, which usage is to be followed? A word can be used in a multiplicity of ways. In John 18:10 ἕλκω is used with μάχαιρα 'to *draw* a sword', in John 21:6 it occurs with δίκτυον 'to *pull* (or *haul*) a net', and in James 2:6 with κριτήρια 'to *drag* before the court'. If usage were to be a guide to the meaning of a word in exegesis, which of the above are to be selected as representing the 'meaning'? The one that suits our purpose best, or a totality transfer incorporating all usages? In either case one would fail to determine the *meaning,* since meaning and usage are not the same.

Besides the fact that meaning operates on the levels of the word, the sentence, and the context—and that these levels require a distinction between understanding, reference, implication, and usage—several kinds (or types) of meaning can further be distinguished. These types of meaning are: cognitive, figurative, emotive, grammatical, encyclopedic, logical, and linguistic. Some of these have been touched upon in previous chapters of this study and will only be briefly commented on here to complete the picture.

Cognitive meanings are those generally thought of as the objects or events signified, that is, the referents in the practical world. Therefore cognitive meanings are often called referential meanings. The cognitive meaning of 'bicycle' signifies the referent, namely that particular kind of vehicle. Thus, people often speak of the literal meaning of a word. The term *referential* should not be confused with *reference,* discussed above. In a sentence such as 'my bicycle has broken and I must fix the thing today', the term 'thing' refers to 'bicycle', but does not mean it, while the referential meaning of 'bicycle' is the particular vehicle concerned. To avoid confusion "cognitive" is perhaps a better term than "referential," though the latter is widely used.

Occasionally people find the idea of a referent problematic. For example, what is the referent involved in 'unicorn'? Has anybody ever seen a unicorn? One may also include other items in this list, namely, fairies, elves, angels, even God. *Referent* is not a particular visible thing, but a reality which has a particular structure and as such may also be said to be part of "our world." And what is more: the meanings of verbal symbols (say, words) are not really the referents, the entities, in the practical world. They are concepts of distinctive features relating to the entities. Thus, 'bicycle' is not the referent as such, but a term signifying a set of distinctive features associated with an object. In the case of 'bicycle', the object happens to be some particular thing in the practical world; in the case of 'fairy' the object likewise is some particular thing in the practical world. It happens that no one has ever seen a fairy, or a unicorn, and so on—yet, these are as real as any other thing in the world. We can even draw pictures of them. Cognitive meaning is, therefore, essentially conceptual.

When Christ, in Luke 13:32, referred to Herod by saying εἴπατε τῇ ἀλώπεκι ταύτῃ "tell that fox," he did not mean to indicate that Herod is a particular kind of wild quadruped. This would be the cognitive meaning of ἀλώπηξ. Only *one* feature, in fact, a supplementary feature associated with the real animal, was held to be common with Herod. This one supplementary feature now becomes the diagnostic feature constituting essentially a new meaning—the metaphorical, or figurative, extension of the cognitive meaning. A figurative meaning builds upon a cognitive meaning, yet constitutes a separate meaning usually belonging to a quite different semantic domain than that of the cognitive meaning. If we were to call somebody 'a fox', the meaning no longer belongs to the domain of (wild) animals, but to that of (bad) people. To go back to the fox as an animal will not be of much help because it depends on which characteristic of the fox was abstracted. In English the focus is on the cunning characteristics of the fox, yet with the ancients it referred to something broader. The fox was a symbol of a base and wicked person—a rascal. At times his cunningness may be emphasized, but in other instances some different feature of a rascal was in mind. The *catena* on Luke 13:32 (Cremer 1967: 110) explained Jesus' description of Herod as a fox as γὰρ τὸ ζῷον ἀεὶ πανοῦργον καὶ δύστροπον "for the animal is always unscrupulous (or, ready for all crimes) and wayward." Therefore the English 'rogue, rascal' will be closer to the Greek than *our* figurative meaning, namely, cunning. The German translation of Luke by Zink gives it as *"dem Fuchs, dem Verderber."*

Before moving on to emotive meaning, a distinction must be made between a figurative meaning and a figurative usage. Both are figurative, but the first is conventionalized, while the latter is more unique, personal, and a feature of imaginative style. For example, in Jude 12 bad people are referred to as "waterless clouds." This is clearly a figurative expression. Clouds without water are useless though they appear to be promising. This imaginative way that the writer describes people is part of his personal style. It is not a stereotyped, general, established expression of Koiné Greek. If, however, such an expression is taken over into popular use, then it would become a figurative meaning and may even change somewhat in significance. In fact, figurative meanings generally develop from figurative usages. Other examples of figurative usage are Matt 23:4 "they make up heavy packs and pile them on men's shoulders," Luke 1:79 "to guide our feet into the way of peace," John 6:54 "he who eats my flesh and drinks my blood," Rom 10:15 "how wonderful are the feet of those who bring good news." In the case of figurative usage, it is generally easy to understand the meaning of the expression. But once an expression becomes stereotyped, the figurative meaning often becomes more difficult to understand. An example is Rev 22:15 where people are called κύνες "dogs." This is a figurative designation in Greek for 'bad people'. Yet this meaning cannot be derived as such from the animal, dog, since, as was said earlier, there are cultures in which it is a compliment to describe someone as a dog. In such a culture the faithfulness of a dog is extended into a figurative meaning, while in Rev 22:15 a feature of wickedness that is associated with the dog is the basis of the figurative meaning. This shows that a figurative meaning is a meaning in its own right to be known beforehand in the same way as any cognitive meaning.

Emotive meaning is concerned with the emotional value attached to words. While cognitive and figurative meanings are more or less "fixed" within a language community, emotive meanings apply to "feelings" associated with words or phrases, and these may be highly individual, or they may apply to particular circumstances only. Thus, in a specific context a word may be strongly colored emotionally, yet not so in another context. This may be illustrated by a situation of strife between A (the favorite) and B, in which A threatens to give B away to a grandparent, and so B replies: "O, granny! You may go and tell granny if you like." Here 'granny' is said with scorn. The word has a strong emotive value for B. Note, however, that the term 'granny' itself has no such emotional value outside this context. Compare this with the term 'profit' for the leaders of labor unions or the directors of companies. In Matt 27:29 βασιλεύς in the mocking by the soldiers (χαῖρε, βασιλεῦ τῶν Ἰουδαίων) has strong emotive value, yet the term as such does not carry any emotive overtones. Though emotive meanings are generally restricted to individuals and situations, some words or phrases may acquire an emotive overtone for a considerable period of time and be used as such by a majority of people. For example, the word 'apartheid' which has become an international term with a highly derogatory emotional value. Such words have moved on towards the status of taboo words, similar to four-letter words that have a *constant* emotional value. The emotive features are now part of the conventional meaning of that word or phrase. Examples in the Greek NT are γεννήματα ἐχιδνῶν (Matt 3:7), υἱὸν γεέννης (Matt 23:15), εἴη εἰς ἀπώλειαν (Acts 8:20), ἀνάθεμα ἔστω (Gal 1:9), and so on.

A word also has grammatical meaning. In Luke 2:7 οὐκ ἦν αὐτοῖς τόπος, the dative indicates that the situation affected the αὐτοί. Though τόπος is the grammatical subject of the sentence, it is semantically the range of the event in which the αὐτοί is involved. This type of grammatical construction highlights the lack of a τόπος. Nida (1964:61) cites the following example to illustrate two possible meanings depending on the grammatical grouping of the words. The sentence 'the fat major's wife' may be read as 'the fat major has a wife', or 'the major has a fat wife' depending on the way in which the constituents are related to one another, and whether 'fat' is taken as a qualification of 'major', or of 'wife'. Nida and Taber (1969: chap. 3) cite several examples in which the same genitive construction is used for different meanings depending on the kernel sentences underlying these constructions in the sentences of which they are a part. In Eph 1:3 θέλημα θεοῦ "the will of God" means 'God wills' while Eph 1:13 λόγος τῆς ἀληθείας "the word of truth" means 'the word is true', and Mark 12:26 ἐν τῇ βίβλῳ Μωϋσέως "in the book of Moses" means 'in the book that Moses wrote'. In Acts 12:2 Ἡρῴδης ἀνεῖλεν Ἰάκωβον μαχαίρῃ, the grammatical functions involved show that Herod is the one performing the act, James the one experiencing it, and the sword is the instrument used.

These examples indicate that grammatical meaning is essentially threefold: the relationship between agents, instruments, locations, affected, etc., and the event or state; the grouping of constituents within a sentence; the qualifications added to entities. Kasher (1972: 317–18) is, therefore, correct when insisting that any semantic theory must necessarily be presented against the background of a syntactic theory, since in any verbal context the syntactic theory is prior to the semantic theory simply because without any syntactic structure we can hardly have an utterance to interpret semantically.

Another type of meaning is encyclopedic meaning, which refers to anything that can be said about something. The word 'bicycle' signifies a vehicle designed for one person, having two wheels in tandem, and propelled physically by the rider himself. These features may be added to in order to define the meaning more precisely, yet we will soon reach a stage when additional information does not really contribute to defining the meaning of the *term* bicycle, but rather describes features of the *object* bicycle. Such features are not diagnostic to determine the *meaning*, that is, to distinguish the word 'bicycle' from other words in the language—and therefore these features (being highly supplementary) are, in fact, encyclopedic. For example, information concerning the colors of bicycles; the size of wheels, tires, gears; the types of seats, handlebars, frames, etc; and data concerning the history of bicycles. In Matt 10:16 doves are referred to as "gentle." This feature is part of the encyclopedic meaning of 'dove' in the ancient world. Encyclopedic meaning may even differ among the general public and specialists. For example, in English a woman of indiscriminate morals may be figuratively called a 'vixen'. This is based on a popular encyclopedic meaning of 'fox', yet zoologists know that foxes are monogamous animals. In the same way 'doves' are often referred to as symbols of peace, yet ornithologists tell us that doves can be quite belligerent.

Finally we may distinguish logical and linguistic meaning. This distinction has been discussed in chapter 2, therefore only one example illustrating the point may suffice at this stage. Nida (1975a: 17) showed that a sentence such as 'a bachelor is an unmarried man' is logically true to its meaning since 'bachelor' and 'unmarried man' both relate to 'human, adult, male, not married'. Therefore the logical meaning of 'bachelor' and 'unmarried man' is the same in this context. However, it would be wrong to conclude that 'bachelor' and 'unmarried man' are linguistically identical in meaning since they may involve significant differences in connotation. Logical meaning is primarily concerned with the truth value of utterances, while linguistic meaning deals with all the features involved in communication.

In the previous paragraphs the problem of meaning was considered with reference to certain *types* of meaning. But meaning may also be considered with reference to certain *relations* of meaning. These relations constitute two different approaches to the problem of meaning. The first approach involves considering *the various meanings of the same lexical unit.* That is, how the meaning of a particular word or phrase may be interpreted in relation to its syntactic and contextual environment. The other approach to meaning involves considering *the related meanings of different lexical units.* That is, how a particular meaning may be presented by different lexical items each focusing on a certain set of features of that particular meaning. These two approaches are concerned with the two different types of relations involved in the problem of meaning. The first deals primarily with the meaning of, say, ξύλον in contexts such as εἰ ἐν τῷ ὑγρῷ ξύλῳ "if they do these things to a green *tree,* what will happen in the case of a dry one?" Luke 23:31; πᾶν σκεῦος ἐκ ξύλου τιμιωτάτου "all kinds of objects made of valuable *wood*" Rev 18:12; ὄχλος μετὰ μαχαιρῶν καὶ ξύλων "a crowd with swords and *clubs*" Mark 14:43; τοὺς πόδας ἠσφαλίσατο αὐτῶν εἰς τὸ ξύλον "fastened their feet in *stocks*" Acts 16:24; Ἰησοῦν ὃν ὑμεῖς διεχειρίσασθε κρεμάσαντες ἐπὶ ξύλου "Jesus, whom you had killed by nailing him to a *cross*" Acts 5:30. Thus, ξύλον occurs in the NT to signify a 'tree' ('a large woody plant'), 'wood' ('part of a plant as a substance'), 'club' ('a weapon used in fighting'), 'stock' ('an instrument to detain a person'), 'cross' ('an instrument of execution'). Though one may think that there exists a significant semantic relationship between these meanings (for instance, that they are all woody by nature), this is essentially of secondary importance. 'Tree' and 'wood' belong to the semantic field of plants, while 'club', 'stocks', and 'cross' belong to the semantic field of artifacts. This is a much more significant feature distinguishing these terms from one another semantically than merely noting that all share the feature of woodiness. Therefore 'tree' and 'wood' are closer in semantic space to each other than to 'club', 'stocks', and 'cross'. Further: 'stocks' and 'cross' are again somewhat closer to each other in semantic space than to 'club', since both relate to instruments used for dealing with criminals—'stocks' as an instrument of binding, 'cross' as a means of execution. Yet these five meanings have much more in common with other lexical items signifying the same meaning respectively than with one another. When ξύλον means 'tree' it shares the same semantic field with δένδρον ('any kind of large woody plant, especially a tree') and ὕλη when ὕλη means a 'forest' (i.e., 'a dense growth of trees covering a relatively large area') or specific trees such as συκῆ 'fig tree', ἐλαία 'olive tree', and the like. These terms all belong to the semantic field of trees: δένδρον being the most generic term, ὕλη adding the feature of "collective", συκῆ, ἐλαία, etc. being specific. This means that between δένδρον, ὕλη, ξύλον, συκῆ, ἐλαία there are many more shared features of meaning than, for example, between ξύλον 'tree', and ξύλον 'club'. Likewise ξύλον 'wood' has more in common with ὕλη when ὕλη means 'a pile of wood', or with φρύγανον 'dry wood', especially 'firewood', or with κάρφος 'a small piece of wood, a splinter', than even with ξύλον 'tree'. In the same way ξύλον 'club' shares the same semantic space with ὅπλον 'weapon', or ῥομφαία 'sword'. When ξύλον means 'stocks', it shares with ζευκτηρία 'bands', σχοινίον 'a rope', δέσμος 'a bond', and so forth. The meaning 'cross', though a figurative extension of 'wood' or perhaps 'tree', is nevertheless a separate meaning belonging to the same semantic field as σταυρός 'cross', and even φραγέλλιον 'whip', in John 2:15, signifying an instrument of punishment. Therefore, the *related* meanings of different lexical units are much closer in semantic space than the *different* meanings of the same lexical unit.

Related meanings reflect *four* basic types which have been proposed by Nida (1975a: chap. 3, 1975c: chap. 1), namely: included, overlapping, complementary, and contiguous relations.

Included relations involve a hierarchical structure. In English the words 'dog' and 'poodle' both indicate dogs. 'Dog' is the general term while 'poodle' is more specific, signifying a particular kind of dog. We may say that the term 'dog' contains 'poodle', and in the field of meaning the terms appear to be hierarchically ordered. Considering the semantic field of animals in the NT, a four-fold division is found: generic, medial, specific, extraspecific. Examples are: ζῷον 'animal' (generic), ἑρπετόν 'reptile' (medial), ὄφις 'snake' (specific), ἔχιδνα 'viper' (extraspecific). This provides the basic hierarchical structure applicable to all kinds of animals. In Mark 1:13 θηρίον is a generic term: καὶ ἦν μετὰ τῶν θηρίων "and he lived there among the animals." Though the reference is probably to wild animals, θηρίον as such applies to wild *and* domesticated animals, any animal—in fact, any living creature not including man. In this usage θηρίόν overlaps with ζῷον in 2 Pet 2:12 οὗτοι δέ, ὡς ἄλογα ζῷα "they are like brute animals." The term ζῷον differs from θηριόν in focusing on the fact that these are living creatures which can move around in contrast with plants, while θηριόν specifies that man is excluded. Another meaning (applying hierarchically to the medical group) of θηριόν is found in James 3:7 πᾶσα γὰρ φύσις θηρίων . . . δαμάζεται "man can tame any animal." Here the meaning applies to quadrupeds, since in the context of James 3:7 θηριόν is distinguished from birds, reptiles, and fishes. The term δαμάζεται shows that the reference is to wild quadrupeds. Thus, we have two meanings for θηριόν in the NT: animal, quadruped. In Heb 12:20 κἂν θηρίον θίγῃ τοῦ ὄρους "if an animal touches the mountain," the meaning is probably generic though the reference would seem to be to domesticated animals that might wander onto the holy mountain. In Acts 28:4, 5 the generic meaning applies in a similar way, yet the reference is to a snake. It is of the utmost importance to see clearly the structure of the semantic field in which a word appears in order to distinguish between its meaning and reference. This can only be done if a fairly large number of contexts in which a word is found is studied with close attention paid to these semantic principles.

In the NT κτῆνος refers to several kinds of animals. In Acts 23:24 κτήνη παραστῆσαι, the reference is to riding animals, in Rev 18:13 κτήνη καὶ πρόβατα indicates cattle, while in Luke 10:34 τὸ ἴδιον κτῆνος is a pack animal, probably a donkey or mule. The context every time contributes in localizing the particular animal concerned. However, a problem occurs in 1 Cor 15:39 ἄλλη μὲν (σάρξ) ἀνθρώπων, ἄλλη δὲ σάρξ κτήνων. From the context we may argue that κτήνων is simply a highly generic expression for all kinds of animals. Yet if the hierarchical structure for terms signifying animals in the NT is known, it will be discovered that κτῆνος, together with θρέμμα, is a medial term for tame animals signifying large domesticated animals, while θρέμμα signifies all types of four-footed domesticated animals, whether large or small. Paul's reference is generic while in the contexts cited above the reference is more specific. The second type of relation between meanings may be described as *overlapping*. This involves what are usually called synonyms. In everyday language the term *synonym* is used to mean 'words with the *same* meaning'. However, this is an incorrect linguistic understanding of this semantic concept. Synonyms are not words that *have* the same meaning, but words that sometimes, or probably quite often, *can be used* for the same meaning. This implies that there are instances where "synonyms" are *not* interchangeable. Since we can hardly, if ever, quote synonymous terms that can be interchanged in each and every context, Nida (1975b: 123) was therefore justified in stating that "it is doubtful if there is ever an instance of complete synonymity." The meanings for which so-called synonymous terms are used do not entirely overlap, for there is always an aspect of meaning that distinguishes them from one another. For example, a '*big* house' and a '*large* house' may be regarded as synonymous in many contexts, yet 'large' may focus on the content of physical dimensions, while 'big' may suggest somewhat more the idea of volume or capacity. A '*huge* house' is indeed a big, or large, house, though 'huge' suggests a more intense concept. A '*huge* house' and a '*gigantic* house' may still signify a shade of difference in that 'gigantic' is even more intense than 'huge'. Sometimes the difference is geographical, as between the Afrikaans terms *wingerdrank* and *wingerdloot* meaning 'vine *shoot*'. Or, the difference may be on the level of language, for example '*dried* prunes' and '*dessicated* prunes'. The latter is more formal, technical—and, in some contexts, pedantic. In other cases one term is used in certain combinations more often than others, like 'much' and 'many' in 'much milk' and 'many apples'. This difference in usage is explained by the fact that 'much' is used with quantities that cannot be easily counted, while 'many' is used with countable items. Yet, semantically, both are concerned with large quantities. Often the difference is a stylistic one: in one situation it will sound better to say 'they presented him with a book' rather than 'they gave him a book'.

To appreciate the finer differences between synonyms, a very intimate knowledge of the language is demanded; and even then, as in the case of native speakers, there is, at times, no mutual agreement. Some would insist that in a particular context only one of two synonyms may be used, while others would regard both as acceptable for that context. Therefore it is often difficult to pinpoint the differences between synonyms in modern languages, and even more so in ancient languages. For example, there is a problem in making a distinction between βόσκω and ποιμαίνω in John 21:15, 16—even if they are translated 'feed my lambs' and 'tend my sheep'. Some scholars believe that in both cases these two words only indicate the activity of 'taking care of animals'. The *TEV* translates these words 'take care of' in both cases. Other scholars assume that βόσκω and ποιμαίνω reflect the same difference as in English between 'feed' and 'tend'. The first is limited to 'eat', or rather 'let them eat', while 'tend' refers to a more embracing action.

A rather difficult case would be the following one, which is found in the NT and concerns the interpersonal activity of welcoming a person by receiving him with friendship and affection: δέχομαι (Matt 10:40), ἀναδέχομαι (Acts 28:7), ἀποδέχομαι (2 Cor 6:17), ὑποδέχομαι (Luke 10:38), ἐπιδέχομαι (3 John 10), εἰσδέχομαι (2 Cor 6:17), προσδέχομαι (Luke 15:2), and παραδέχομαι (Acts 15:4). There may be subtle differences between these terms, and the ancient speakers presumably would have sensed them, but it is not possible to distinguish between them with our present knowledge.

In other instances, as for example καταβραβεύω in Col 2:18 and συκοφαντέω in Luke 19:8, a difference may be noted. Both are concerned with the meaning 'to take advantage of someone by illegal or quasi-illegal means', though συκοφαντέω may focus somewhat more on the misleading that accompanies the event. This distinction is based on the fact that in classical Greek συκοφαντέω is often associated with blackmail. Probably this association continued in later times to be part of the connotative meaning of συκοφαντέω, but it is difficult to determine precisely whether this feature is stronger in συκοφαντέω than in καταβραβεύω.

When it happens that two words become more and more interchangeable, and so move towards becoming complete synonyms, experience has shown that one of the words will usually disappear from use, or acquire a new meaning. In Afrikaans this is presently the case with *kar* and *motor* when signifying a motor vehicle. Earlier *kar* designated a carriage drawn by animals, while *motor* applied to an automobile. Later both were used for an automobile, and eventually *kar* became the generally used term while *motor* acquired an emotive overtone as a snobbish term when used of an automobile. At the present time, however, *motor* is generally used for a source of power, in particular an electric one. Another kind of relation can be described as *complementary*. This is of importance in cases of opposites (often called "polar opposites," or "antonyms") such as 'low/high', 'hot/cold', 'bad/good', and the like. The two words in each group share certain features of meaning, but differ radically in one aspect, namely, that one is the negation of the other—and so each may be explained by the other. Complementary relations also include sets such as 'buy/sell', 'lend/borrow', and so on. These are not strictly polar opposites. Nida (1975a: 32–34) called these "conversives" or "reciprocals," since they focus on the roles played by the participants while the activity in itself involves many of the same features. A third type of complementary relation involves sequences where one is the reverse of the other, such as 'bind/loose', 'estrange/reconcile', 'tie/unite'. These terms are "reversives."

There is also a fourth type of relation which is certainly the most important one, since it involves almost any word in its relation to other words. Nida referred to this type of relationship as *"contiguous."* That is to say, words do not exist in isolation, but are always related to other words. Words such as 'water', 'rain', 'moisture', 'ice', 'snow', and 'hail' are related through each being a specific item that can be subsumed under the label 'natural substances', with 'water' as the generic term. Words like 'chair', 'table', 'bed', and 'wardrobe', are related, since they are items of furniture. 'Bench' and 'stool' are also items of furniture, yet they link more closely with 'chair' (as items of furniture on which people sit) than with the others. Terms like διαθήκη ('covenant, pact'), δικαιόω, δικαίωσις, δικαιοσύνη ('to be put right with, be in a right relation with'), ἀσύνθετος ('to not keep a promise'), and the idiom δεξιὰς δίδωμι ('to give right hands, i.e., to make a covenant') are all related to each other as interpersonal events of association constituting a set of meanings, that is, a semantic field, which may be defined as 'to establish or confirm a relationship'. Words such as πάλαι, ἔκπαλαι and the phrases ἀπ᾽ αἰῶνος and ἀφ᾽ ἡμερῶν ἀρχαίων, all meaning 'long ago', constitute a semantic field, or domain, along with items such as the idiom γενεὰ ἀρχαῖα ('ancient generations', i.e., 'very long ago', as in Acts 15:21), πρεσβύτερος ('a person of ancient times', as in Heb 11:2) and the polar opposite καινότερον ('latest', as in Acts 17:21). These terms are related through each being an item of time signifying a time prior to the event of the discourse. In like manner all the words used in a language can be related with one another. These relations obviously become more and more tenuous the further a word is from where one starts. Thus 'father' relates closely with 'mother', 'daughter', 'son', 'cousin', and so on, as terms indicating familial relationships, but 'father' is also related in a wider sense to 'man', since both belong to the domain of human beings in contrast to animals or plants. Words, therefore, relate to some other words in a close relationship which is in fact part of a wider relationship in which many other words are included. The terms 'humans', 'plants', 'animals' can be subdivided into 'men', 'women', 'children' (which may be further subdivided into smaller sets including items such as 'baby', 'stepchild', 'orphan', etc.); 'trees', 'bushes', and 'fruit', (again with a number of subdivisions); and 'quadrupeds', 'fishes', and 'birds' (along with subdivisions). But 'humans', 'plants', and 'animals' may be themselves subdivisions of a larger domain, namely, 'living creatures'. And 'living creatures' can combine with 'artifacts' ('chair', 'table', 'knife', 'bowl', etc.) and 'constructions' ('house', 'temple', etc.) and many more, to constitute a large overall domain of 'objects' in contrast to 'events'. Distinctions such as these always turn upon common characteristics in opposition to distinctive characteristics. Finally, an extensive survey of all the items in a language will lead to the uncovering of three basic semantic categories: objects, events, and abstracts. These represent the most comprehensive categories in which meanings can be distributed. Therefore, they are called *semantic categories* in contrast to *grammatical categories,* which comprise the so-called parts of speech: nouns, verbs, adjectives, adverbs, articles, and so on.

Some English and NT Greek examples can be used to illustrate the notion of semantic categories. In a sentence such as 'he eats many apples', 'he' is an object, 'eats' is an event, 'many' an abstract, and 'apples' is again an object. Objects are entities such as 'apples', 'mountains', 'iron', 'moon', 'swamp', 'water', 'cup', 'sword', 'ship', 'tree', 'lion', 'flower', 'angel', and so on. Events include all kinds of activities such as 'rain', 'sleep', 'smell', 'longing', 'memory', 'dialogue', 'command', 'visit', 'jump', 'hit', 'sacrifice', 'sin', 'forgiveness', 'sorrow', and 'love'. Abstracts describe qualities or capacities of objects and/or events, plus describing relations between objects and/or events. Relations are a specific group of abstracts often considered for practical purposes as a fourth group. This is a useful distinction since relations constitute a large group among the abstracts and have a peculiarity of their own, but they are actually only a particular subset of the category of abstracts. Abstracts are terms such as 'red', 'ugly', 'fast', 'rich', 'weak', 'old', 'many', 'three', and 'yesterday'. Relations are abstracts that indicate position, such as 'above', 'around', 'behind', and 'in'; or deixis, such as 'this' or 'that'; or they describe the logical relations, such as 'so that', 'but', and 'although'.

The following Greek terms represent sometime abstracts that indicate duration of time: διηνεκής ('always'), αἰώιος ('eternal'), ἀεὶ ('always'), διὰ παντός ('continuous'). By considering these terms in such a grouping, their similarities and differences become clearer. Among these terms αἰώνιος is used in the NT as an absolute term for uninterrupted duration. The other three may be used as synonyms for each other. In this case the focus is also on the duration of time, yet they allow for an interruption in the passage of time. Their individual differences can be described as existing only on the stylistic level, while διηνεκής occurs in NT usage only as part of the phrase εἰς τὸ διηνεκής (Heb 7:3). The phrase as such is merely a more elaborate expression without any distinction of meaning when compared to διηνεκής.

Among the event words are χάρις, εὐχαριστέω, εὐχαριστία, εὐλογέω, ἐξομολογέομαι, and ἀνθομολογέομαι. These words constitute a semantic field when used for the meaning of 'to express thanks'. As such they operate within the field of communication. It is noteworthy that several words within a single field can be used to render the same meaning. If languages had only one word for each meaning, semantic analysis would have been made much easier, but this would have made language a very tedious and dull instrument. Indeed, it is through there being so many different ways to communicate a meaning that levels of style, subtleties of expression, wordplay, and the like, make language such a plastic instrument.

Chapter 9

Semantics Is More Than the Meaning of Words

J. C. Nyíri (1971) maintained that "a word has no meaning independently from the way in which it is connected to other words." This statement underlines the fact that semantics crosses word boundaries, as C. Rabin (1958) demonstrated by showing that 'Jack and Jill' is not a threefold reference to 'Jack' + 'sees' + 'Jill', but a unit in which the three elements are in a relationship to each other. As a consequence of this the following transformations are justified: 'Jill is seen by Jack', 'Jill is visible to Jack', 'Jack's view of Jill'. In each case Jack is the experiencer, while Jill is the affected. The occasion relating the experiencer to the affected is the sensory event of seeing. These relationships actually constitute our understanding of these sentences.

Meaning is not merely a product of the additions of the supposed individual meanings of the separate words constituting a sentence. We may use exactly the same words as in 'this woman is a judge' and 'this judge is a woman' without necessarily conveying the same meaning. On the other hand, in transformations such as 'I hit the dog/the dog is being hit by me', the event is the same in both cases though we have used different words. The fact that one sentence is active and the other passive does not change the relations between the elements. The only thing changed is the focus. In the active construction the focus is on the agent, while in the passive construction it is on the experiencer. In the NT a passive construction is often used to avoid directly mentioning the name of God because of the speaker's reverence for the word. So in cases when the context clearly points to God as the subject the passive

is used. Examples of this are the passives found at the beginning of the
Beatitudes from the Sermon on the Mount, Matthew 5: αὐτοὶ
παρακληθήσονται "they will be comforted" = 'God will comfort
them', αὐτοὶ χορτασθήσονται "they will be satisfied" = 'God will
satisfy them', υἱοὶ θεοῦ κληθήσονται "they will be called children of
God" = 'God will call them his children'.

Meaning is very much a matter that depends on the relations among
words (or their combinations), and their grammatical structure. It is
also dependent on the situation of the utterance. Semantics is
therefore concerned with more than simply the meanings of words.
When semantics is discussed, *all* the things that contribute to meaning
must be explored and not just the semantics of words. All language
units that have meaning are of concern to semantics—words, phrases,
sentences, paragraphs, and so forth, even the total document or
narrative. From a practical point of view it seems rather impossible to
start immediately with the largest units, although this is the actual
starting point in language performance. A speaker or writer naturally
has something to say, that is, a theme which is worked out by using
paragraphs, sentences, words, and so on. In analyzing what a speaker
or document actually intended to convey it is merely practical to begin
with the smaller units because they are more manageable, but we must
work up to the structure as a whole.

In a sentence such as 'he walks' there are only two elements related
to each other with no other possible combinations in linking 'he' to
'walks', that is, he walks. When the sentence is extended, the words
are related in such a way that some are closer to others in that any
addition to a sentence such as 'he walks' will necesarily involve linking
this addition to either 'he' or 'walks'. In the sentence 'he walks away',
the element 'away' is a restriction defining 'walks'. There is a closer
relation between 'walks' and 'away' than between 'he' and 'away'. This
may be represented as: he walks away.

The question that immediately arises is why such differences in
relations between the words of the sentence exist. Could there not be a
close relation between 'he' and 'walks' with 'away' taken as just an
additional unit, that is, he walks away.

Psychologically this second description seems more acceptable, yet one of the basic rules of linguistics is that psychological judgments must never be preferred over linguistic ones. This is simply because such judgments are highly subjective, and may differ from person to person. The grouping of elements is therefore not to be based on subjective intuition, but upon linguistic criteria. This linguistic basis is nothing more than the fact that the most fundamental division of a sentence that can be determined from an analysis of a great number of sentences is that into a nominal and a verbal part. Therefore, utterances such as 'up there', or 'in the basket' (often occurring in conversation) are by no means typical. A typical sentence consists of combinations such as 'he walks', or 'Nancy sleeps'. This combination (often referred to as subject and predicate) is the major characteristic of sentences found in languages all over the world. The sentence 'he walks' may, therefore, be analyzed as 'he' = nominal element, and 'walks' = verbal element. Schematically this can be shown as:

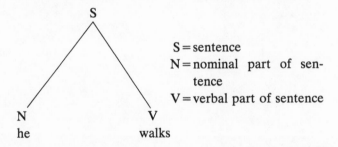

S = sentence
N = nominal part of sentence
V = verbal part of sentence

If the sentence 'John walks away' is divided, the word 'away' belongs to the verbal part because it extends the verbal element. It is not defining 'John'. In this way larger units can be analyzed as:

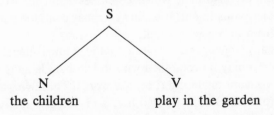

The group 'play in the garden' may be further analyzed as having 'the' + 'garden' as a smaller unit which links with 'in' to constitute the phrase 'in the garden'. This may be presented as:

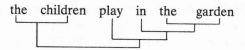

or it may be presented as:

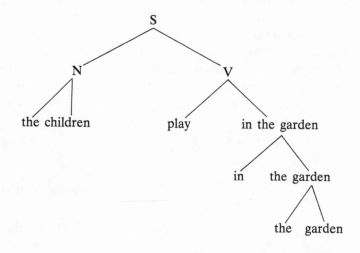

This principle is the same as that used by Chomsky in his famous book *Syntactic Structures* (1957), and since then in all transformational grammars. The groupings of elements which belong together may also be referred to as *immediate constituents*. Thus, 'the garden' is an immediate constituent which combines with 'in' to form a larger immediate constituent. In this way we may continue until the sentence is built up into a whole unit.

In many languages a substitute for the nominal element ('I, you, we, she', etc.) may be combined with the verbal element to constitute a single conventional form (i.e., one word). Thus 'we walk' is normally one word in Greek, βαδίζομεν, and yet this one-word sentence overtly displays the nominal (in the personal ending μεν) and the verbal (in the stem βαδιζ) elements. Yet if we wish to analyze a term such as βαδίζει, the ending (-ει) is ambiguous since it does not state whether the nominal element is 'he' or 'she'. A form such as βαδίζει, if analyzed according to our model, must be presented as:

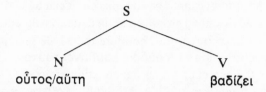

In most cases the nominal element will be completed by the context. An example would be John 13:20 ὁ ἐμὲ λαμβάνων λαμβάνει τὸν πέμψαμτά με. This sentence has seven words, yet the meaning of the sentence is not a linear addition of the elements but is based on the structural relationship between the elements. If we merely join the meaning of each word together the following will result: 'the me receiving, receives the sending me'. R. Brown (1958) has shown how if the sentence 'he invites people to a feast' is translated as the sum of the total number of words into Nootka, a language of Vancouver Island, something like 'boiled eaters go for (he) does' will result. The French sentence *comment allez-vous?* gives 'how are you going?' but again the meaning is not a question about how a person is going on a journey. The expression is used to enquire after someone's well-being. De Mauro (1964: 40) quoted an example between English and Japanese. The sentence 'the spirit is willing but the flesh is weak' was given to a translation machine to be rendered into Japanese word by word. Once this was done, the sentence was again given to the machine to be translated back into English. The result was: 'there is some good whisky but the roast beef is mediocre'. The machine was only programmed to translate words without considering their relations to each other. This resulted in a choice of meanings assigned to each word which did not account for the syntactic construction involved. It treated the sentence as if the words were isolated units.

The Greek sentence from John 13:20, quoted earlier, can be divided into three major groups:

ὁ ἐμὲ λαμβάνων   λαμβάνει   τὸν πέμψαντά με.

To determine the immediate units of this sentence, the words that have the closest relationship to each other are first grouped together. Since ὁ ἐμὲ λαμβάνων may be replaced by a single word like οὗτος or οὐδείς, without altering the overall syntactic structure, whereas ὁ ἐμὲ λαμβάνων λαμβάνει cannot be so replaced, it can be said that ὁ ἐμὲ λαμβάνων is an extended group, an immediate constituent. The same is true for τὸν μέμψαντά με. Therefore the whole sentence may be replaced by substitution with οὐδεὶς λαμβάνει τοῦτον. The nuclear structure of the sentence being agent-action-affected is in no way altered. The sentence οὐδεὶς λαμβάνει τοῦτον is a simpler constructional unit of the same type as ὁ ἐμὲ λαμβάνων λαμβάνει τὸν πέμψαντά με. The simpler sentence with its three words can be analyzed as: οὐδεὶς λαμβάνει τοῦτον

This can also be represented as:

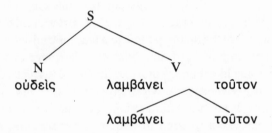

In the longer sentence ὁ ἐμὲ λαμβάνων is an extended structural counterpart of οὐδείς, and so τὸν πέμψαντά με of τοῦτον. Thus, the immediate constituents of the longer sentence can be arranged as:

The phrase ὁ ἐμὲ λαμβάνων is a participial construction that is in itself a nominalization presenting the subject of the total sentence. As a nominalization it is based on the sentence (οὗτος) λαμβάνει ἐμέ 'he accepts me'. The change from 'he who accepts me' to 'he accepts me', or the reverse, is called a transformation. In this sense the term *transformation* will be used in this study. Transformation, therefore, refers to different structures related to the same meaning. The phrase ὁ ἐμὲ λαμβάνων can now be structurally schematized as:

ὁ   ἐμὲ   λαμβάνων   structurally related to

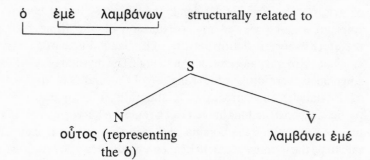

N   V
οὗτος (representing   λαμβάνει ἐμέ
the ὁ)

Of these two structures (οὗτος) γαμβάνει ἐμέ is the closest in form to the simple sentence pattern consisting of a subject and predicate. The phrase ὁ ἐμὲ λαμβάνων involves nominalization of this simple pattern and is thus a more sophisticated construction of which (οὗτος) λαμβάνει ἐμέ is the simplest form. On the basis of this point of view we may say that ὁ ἐμὲ λαμβάνων is based on (οὗτος) λαμβάνει ἐμέ. Therefore, if ὁ ἐμὲ λαμβάνων is found in a text, we may say that this surface structure is based on a deep structure, namely, (οὗτος) λαμβάνει ἐμέ. *Deep structure* refers to the basic syntactic pattern in which a meaning is expressed, while *surface structure* refers to the particular form in which a meaning is expressed in a text. It stands to reason that when a sentence such as 'he accepts me' occurs in this form in a text, the surface structure is in the same form as the underlying deep structure.

The above explanation also applies to τὸν πέμψαντά με and therefore the whole sentence may be analyzed as:

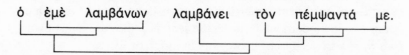

ὁ   ἐμὲ   λαμβάνων   λαμβάνει   τὸν   πέμψαντά   με.

Rulon Wells (1947) argued that a sentence such as 'the King of England opened Parliament' is structurally identical to 'John worked' because 'the King of England' is structurally an extension of 'John' and 'opened Parliament' an extension of 'worked'. Consequently the basic division is found between 'England' and 'opened', and not between 'opened' and 'Parliament'. It is clear that the meaning of the sentence is not determined merely by the individual words, but by the grouping of words. 'The King of England' can also be divided because 'of England' can be viewed as an extension of 'the King'. 'King' is therefore a shortened form of 'King of England'. Put another way, 'of England' is merely an extension of 'King'. The division of 'the King of England' is therefore not the 'King' + 'of England', but 'the' + 'King of England'. This structural relationship is comparable to the participial constructions in the Greek sentence quoted above. In both these constructions the nominalization implies an agent that can be said to be the nominal element of a sentence having ἐμὲ λαμβάνει and ἔπεμψέ με as verbal elements. The participial constructions represent embedded sentences which may be illustrated by the following diagram:

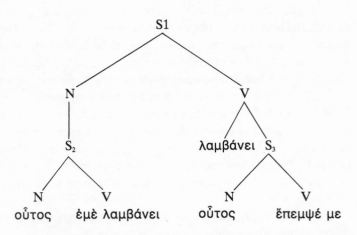

By describing the relationships between the words of an expression we may often discern ambiguous constructions. One of the famous examples in modern linguistics is the sentence 'they are flying planes' which can be analyzed in two totally different ways:

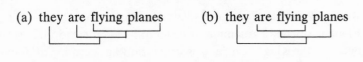

(a) they are flying planes	(b) they are flying planes
= 'they are planes that are flying'	= 'they are causing planes to fly'

Another example is Rom 1:17 ὁ δὲ δίκαιος ἐκ πίστεως ζήσεται which can be analyzed in two ways:

(a)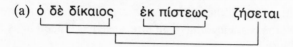

= "he who through faith is righteous shall live" (*RSV*)

= "he who is put right with God through faith shall live" (*GNB*)

(b)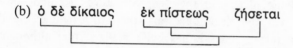

= "the just shall live by faith" (*KJV*)

= "the upright man finds life through faith" (*JB*)

These ambiguous constructions clearly show that a particular surface structure such as ὁ δὲ δίκαιος ἐκ πίστεως ζήσεται, for example, can be related to quite different deep structures. One of the important achievements of modern linguistics is its demonstration of the need to distinguish between these two levels in language. To appreciate the value of this distinction for the study of semantics, a more detailed discussion is necessary.

In Eph 1:7 ἐν ᾧ ἔχομεν τὴν ἀπολύτρωσιν διὰ τοῦ αἵματος αὐτοῦ, we have a syntactic structure in which a preposition ἐν combines with the relative pronoun ᾧ as the instrument of the verb ἔχομεν having τὴν ἀπολύτρωσιν as its object. This is followed by another prepositional phrase διὰ τοῦ αἵματος, also an instrument linked to ἔχομεν, while αὐτοῦ is a genitive of possession qualifying αἵματος. What has now been described is the surface structure of the sentence, and from these grammatical relations Eph 1:7 is taken to mean "by whom we have redemption through his blood." However, if the sentence is analyzed according to its deep structure relationships we understand the sentence as 'God sets us free because Christ died for us'. How do we arrive at this point? The surface structure shows the grammatical relations which are important to the meaning of the sentence, yet only a part of the meaning meets the eye, so to speak. A deep structure analysis will show even more clearly that semantics involves relationships rather than merely words and their meanings. That is to say, the real meaning of an utterance lies hidden in its deep structure to a large extent.

Initially this approach has led to the assumption that the deep structure is the only level of meaning, and this led to the surface structure being ignored because it was considered only an external manifestation of the deep structure. Consequently the thought was entertained that the surface structure contributed nothing to the meaning of an utterance but was only a mere bearer of the real expression lying hidden in the deep structure. To understand a sentence it was therefore necessary only to examine the deep structure. In recent times it has been realized that although the semantic information is derived from the deep structure, it must not be interpreted apart from the surface structure. This conviction rests upon the fact that when something is said, every language presents a number of ways in which to say it. The *choice* of surface structures is in itself a semantic one. The chosen surface structure is essentially the one that renders the deep structure in the best way. The *manner* in which something is said, is indeed part of the semantic analysis. This has already been illustrated above in our discussion of active and passive constructions. Each passage has to be thoroughly investigated so as to determine whether the chosen surface structure is purposeful or not. If there is no obvious focus to be distinguished then this could mean that the author did not want certain nuances to be attached to his words. When nuances are attached, as is often the case, they are certainly important to the semantic analysis. In other words, meaning is determined by (a) the grouping of words and their semantic relations to each other, and (b) the choice of structure when there is more than one possible form available in the language.

The expression 'died for us' given as the deep structure for διὰ τοῦ αἵματος αὐτοῦ (Eph 1:7), can have other surface structures, such as ὑπὲρ ὑμῶν ἀπέθανε, τὴν ζωὴν ὑμῖν ἀπέδωκε, ὑπὲρ ὑμῶν ἐσταυρώθη, and so on. The reason why Paul chose διὰ τοῦ αἵματος was to express the death of Christ as a sacrifice. The meaning lies primarily in the notion of Christ's *death* contained in the deep structure, since αἵμα is here used in its figurative sense. However, the surface structure by which this was expressed contains associations that his death is a fulfillment of the OT sacrificial atonement. On the other hand this should not be stressed since the essential meaning of αἷμα in Eph 1:7 is not 'blood', but 'death'. 1 John 1:7 τὸ αἷμα 'Ιησοῦ καθαρίζει ἡμᾶς ἀπὸ πάσης ἁμαρτίας does not mean that the blood as a liquid reconciles our sins. It refers to the death of Christ—the whole deed of atonement of which the blood is a symbol. This specific surface structure was probably chosen because others, such as ἀπέθανε, do not render as well the total intention of the author. In such cases it must be discovered whether the surface structure really does point to the focus because it could easily be a stereotype that does not have its original nuance. The manner in which the surface structure appears is determined by the entire paragraph in which it occurs rather than the individual words. The purpose of the arrangement of sentences and paragraphs is to bring out the meaning of the whole text, and to attain this purpose the surface structure does play a role. This role will be discussed in the next chapter. At present the concern is with the way in which the deep structure is relevant to the understanding of words and phrases.

With regard to the surface structure it is not merely the structure that is important, but the choice of a specific structure. This means that if the author wishes to say something (deep structure) he will choose a specific form (surface structure) in which to say it. There is no need to see an opposition between the surface and deep structures. They are part of one process. If the deep structure is investigated then the meaning is uncovered, and the outer form of the language, the surface structure, will help us to better understand this meaning. In Eph 1:7 the choice of words forms part of this process. The beginning words ἐν ᾧ indicate that Christ is in focus. If it is translated "God sets us free because Christ died for us" then Christ would have to be accentuated.

Leaving behind the matter of focus for a while, the role of the deep structure in semantic analysis will now be considered in detail to illustrate further that semantics is concerned with more than merely the meaning of words. In Eph 1:13 the words τὸ εὐαγγέλιον τῆς σωτηρίας ὑμῶν "the gospel of your salvation" immediately raises the question what the meaning of the group τῆς σωτηρίας ὑμῶν would be. This is the same as asking, what is the deep structure of which this word group is the surface form? The word σωτηρίας is a noun in surface structure, but semantically it is concerned with an event, namely 'save'. This event is closely related to ὑμῶν since the genitive form ὑμῶν links grammatically to σωτηρίας. The phrase 'your salvation' (i.e., 'your saving') can be grammatically analyzed in two ways, (a) subjective as 'you save (something or someone)', or (b) objective as '(something or someone) saves you'. The connection of this group with τὸ εὐαγγέλιον results in making (b) more probable than (a) since (a) does not make sense in the context in which Eph 1:13 appears. The something or someone of (b) can now be identified as τὸ εὐαγγέλιον which means 'good news'. This will now give us the deep structure: 'the good news saves you'. However, 'good news' is itself an event. The agent behind the event of saving can therefore not be the good news as such. Paul brings the good news, but it is God that saves. The expression τὸ εὐαγγέλιον τῆς σωτηρίας ὑμῶν actually means: 'the good news that I bring proclaims that God saves you'. This is the deep structure behind Eph 1:13. Or perhaps this should be called an intermediate stage of the deep structure, since the true deep structure, as indicated below, is simply subject-verb (-object).

An expression such as 'the good news saves you' is another way of saying 'the good news of your salvation'. The two expressions have the same meaning, or rather, render the same thought. They can be described as transformations of each other. The closer a transformation is to the basic sentence pattern the easier it is to comprehend the meaning. Thus the expression ὁ λόγος τῆς ἀληθείας belongs to a more complicated level of construction than does its transformation ὁ λόγος ἐστιν ἀληθής.

The expression τὸ εὐαγγέλιον τῆς σωτηρίας ὑμῶν can be schematized as:

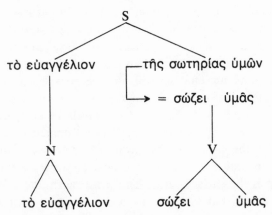

Therefore the surface structure τὸ εὐαγγέλιον τῆς σωτηρίας ὑμῶν has as its deep structure a pattern which coincides structurally with a sentence such as 'I see him', in other words, a subject plus predicate with object: τὸ εὐαγγέλιον σώζει ὑμᾶς.

In the same way John 15:15 can be analyzed:

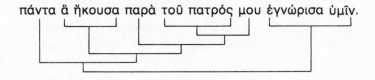

The part πάντα . . . μου is the object of ἐγνώρισα ὑμῖν with ἅ . . . μου as an extension of πάντα. We may rewrite the construction as:

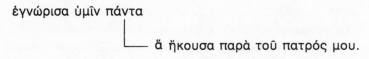

The basic part of the sentence is πάντα ἐγνώρισα ὑμῖν and can be schematized as:

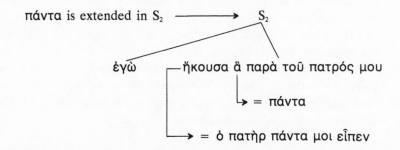

In other words, the deep structure of John 15:15 contains two kernel sentences: 'my father told me everything'/'I told you it'. Although the distinction between surface and deep structure belongs to modern linguistics, it is not so "new" as it may appear. Chomsky (1965:199) admitted this by referring to von Humboldt's 'outer form' and 'inner form' of language. In recent philosophy terms such as 'depth grammar' and 'surface grammar' are familiar as, for example, in Wittgenstein (1953:168) where the terms *'Tiefengrammatik'* and *'Oberflächengrammatik'* are found. Postal (1964) used similar terminology, as can also be seen in the title of his article "Underlying and Superficial Linguistic structures." Chomsky (1965: 199, 1966) even reasoned that the basic idea of these two levels of language can be traced as far back as the *Grammaire générale et raisonnée* of Port-Royal, since it distinguished between "what man thinks" and "what man says." Dinneen (1967: 382) illustrated this with the following example: 'The invisible God created the visible world'. This is the form in which this stretch of communication is *uttered,* but it is *understood* because in it we think of, (1) 'God created the world', (2) 'God is invisible', (3) 'the world is visible'. The surface structure is then nothing else but a transformation of the deep structure.

The two levels of language are not only restricted to sentence and word groups. Individual words also have a surface and deep structure. This was partially touched on in our discussion of εὐαγγελία and σωτηρία above. Grammatically they are nouns and can appear in surface structure as the subject, object, complement, etc. Yet in their deep structure they belong to the semantic domain of events. The semantic word classes have been discussed in chapter 8 and need not be repeated here. In the sentence quoted above the term 'invisible' in the phrase 'the invisible God' is in its deep structure an *event* to which the features of negation plus potentiality are added: 'that which cannot be seen'. Though it describes a quality of God in surface structure, it is in an adjectival form qualifying God, and yet in deep structure it conveys the meaning: 'no one can see God'.

To illustrate these categories the following examples are cited to demonstrate the deep structure relationships and to make explicit all the implicit information contained in them through a reconstruction of the basic underlying kernel sentences:

(a) τὸ βάπτισμα τὸ 'Ιωάννου   "the baptism of John" (Matt
   | | | | 21:25).
  A   E   A   O

The articles (τὸ) are *abstracts*, being deictic elements making βάπτισμα specific. The term βάπτισμα indicates an *event*, and therefore points to the action of baptizing; 'Ιωάννου is an *object* that can either be the agent of or the one affected by the action 'to baptize'. The surface structure, formulated as 'the baptism of John', can therefore be said to have two deep structures: 'John baptizes (people)', or '(someone) baptizes John'. From the context of Matt 21:25 it is clear that John is the implied agent, and so the text can be restated as 'Ιωάννης βαπτίζει 'John baptizes'. Constructions such as βάπτισμα 'Ιωάννου in which two nouns appear in the surface structure where one is in the genitive case (while these nouns belong to the object and event class respectively as far as their deep structure is concerned), can be better understood if the semantic parts of speech are reduced to transformations which make their kernel structure explicit. For example:

θέλημα θεοῦ "the will of God" (Eph 1:1) = 'God wills', ἡ ἐντολὴ τοῦ θεοῦ "the command of God" (Mark 7:8) = 'God commands', τὸ πνεῦμα τῆς ἐπαγγελίας τὸ ἅγιον "the Holy Spirit of promise" (Eph 1:13) = 'the Holy Spirit which God promised' = 'God promised the Holy Spirit'. All these examples contain an *object* with an *event*. In the case of the first two 'God' is the agent of the event, while in Eph 1:13 'Holy Spirit' is the affected. When an *object* word is found with an *event* word, as above, it must be determined from the context whether the object is the agent of the event, or is affected by the event, or is the experiencer of the event as in βάπτισμα 'Ιωάννου above.

(b) βάπτισμα μετανοίας "baptism of repentance" (Mark 1:4).

E	E

In this example we likewise have nouns in a genitive construction as in (a) above, but now both are event words in deep structure. The agent, affected, or experiencer of the events must be determined only from the context. In the case of βάπτισμα the context of Mark 1:4 shows that people experience baptism, that is, have themselves baptized. In the case of μετανοία the context points to people being the agents, that is, people repent. A very important decision involved in a construction like βάπτισμα μετανοίας is which of the two events occurs first; or do they occur simultaneously? Often in such constructions the term in the genitive occurred first. In other words, βάπτισμα μετανοίας means 'people repent and have themselves baptized'. This is also the case in ὑπακοὴ πίστεως "obedience of faith" (Rom 1:5) = 'people believe and (then) obey'. In Acts 20:24 τὸ εὐαγγέλιον τῆς χάριτος "the good news of grace" two subjects are involved: Paul is the one who brings good news, while God shows kindness. The relationship between these two events is different from that expressed in βάπτισμα μετανοίας and ὑπακοὴ πίστεως. In the case of τὸ εὐαγγέλιον τῆς χάριτος the kindness that God shows is the content of the good news. Therefore it means 'I bring you good news that God shows kindness'. In 2 Cor 1:12 τὸ μαρτύριον τῆς συνειδήσεως "the testimony of conscience" applies to one subject, and yet the relationship between the events is quite different from the above. Here the two events are perhaps coterminous: we know and this knowledge assures us—unless we insist that the assurance is based on the knowledge, and therefore the event in the genitive comes first.

(c) τὸ στερέωμα τῆς πίστεως ὑμῶν　　"the steadfastness of
　　｜　　　｜　　　｜　　　｜　　　｜　　　your faith" (Col 2:5).
　　A　　A　　A　　E　　O

In this example an abstract (στερέωμα) occurs with an event word (πίστεως) in a genitive construction. The abstract qualifies the event, that is, your faith is steadfast, you believe with a steadfast faith. In other words, you believe with a belief not qualified by change or doubt. Similarly εἰς ἔπαινον δόξης τῆς χάριτος αὐτοῦ "to the praise of the glory of his grace" involves δόξης as an abstract with τῆς χάριτος as accompanying genitive, meaning 'his grace is glorious', that is, 'wonderful'. And since χάριτος is an event word having God as agent, we may render the phrase as 'God shows us his wonderful kindness'. The term ἔπαινον is an event word having people as agents along with εἰς, an abstract indicating a relation of purpose. The whole phrase therefore means essentially 'so that we may praise the wonderful kindness God bestows on us'.

(d) τὸ πνεῦμα τῆς ἀληθείας "the Spirit of truth" (John 14:17).
   | | | |
  A   O   A   A

In this example we have an object word combined with an abstract in the genitive case indicating that ἀληθείας is a quality of πνεῦμα, that is, 'the Spirit is true'. A comparable case would be ὁ υἱός μου ὁ ἀγαπητός μου "my beloved son" (2 Pet 1:17). In surface structure ἀγαπητός is a qualification of υἱός, in fact, an adjective. Yet, in deep structure ἀγαπητός is an event word plus the features of person and state of being, that is, 'he who is loved'. The feature "state of being" is in itself an abstract semantic aspect which allows us to define ἀγαπητός as an abstract event (usually designated EA since the *event* is dominant). "State of being" is essentially equivalent to a passive construction in surface structure. This may be presented as 'the one who is loved'. The word μου refers to an object (it is, in fact, an object substitute), which is linked to ἀγαπητός in a genitive construction which, in this case, is the agent of the event of loving, 'the one loved by me', that is, 'the one whom I love'. From the context we know that μου refers to God. The total phrase, therefore, means 'this is my son whom I love'.

(e) ἐγώ εἰμι ἡ ἀνάστασις καὶ ἡ ζωή "I am the resurrection and
  | | | | | | | the life" (John 11:25).
  O A A   E   A A E

Here we have again two event words as in (b) above, but now linked by an abstract of conjunction joining these events together. The term εἰμί is an abstract of state signifying what the object (ἐγώ) is. This 'what' is stated in the two event words. The ἐγώ refers to Christ, and therefore Christ is the ἀνάστασις and the ζωή. The event ἀνάστασις is a causative denoting the event of causing (people) to rise (from death). Similarly ζωή involves the claim that Christ is the one who 'eventuates' life, that is, who causes people to live. The relationship between the two events shows that ζωή is the content which results from ἀνάστασις. The whole sentence can therefore be transformed into 'I am the one who revives people and gives them life'. Resurrection thus means to receive life! Another example of this type of construction is Rom 1:5 ἐλάβομεν χάριν καὶ ἀποστολήν "I received grace and apostleship." The event word χάριν (which means 'privilege' in this context) has God as the agent, that is, 'God gives a privilege'. In the case of ἀποστολήν the event involves working or acting as an apostle (that is, a special messenger). The one who does it is Paul, the experiencer of ἐλάβομεν. The apostleship is the content resulting from the privilege. Rom 1:5 can then be presented as 'God gave me the privilege to be his special messenger'.

The example of ἀγαπητός in (d) above was analyzed as a complex, that is an abstract and an event, or as it was put, an abstract built upon an event (EA). The term ἀπόστολος in (e) above is in reality also a semantic complex since it refers to a person (O) and at the same time an event (E). We may designate ἀπόστολος as EO, but since the event is dominant it can be considered, like ἀγαπητός to be primarily an event. In the same way δῶρον 'gift' may be said to be an event-object, i.e., 'that which is given'. However, the event 'to give' is primary, while the something (O) given is secondary. Sometimes words can be very complex in deep structure, for example, ἀποκαταλλάσσω 'to cause (A) reconciliation (E) between (R)', yet the focus is on the event. In the case of ἁγιάζων, 'he (O) who makes (A = cause) pure (A)', the focus is on the moral quality. Usually only the focal aspect is designated when classifying terms.

In order to distinguish between the surface and deep structure of a continuous stretch of language, the following example may be used:

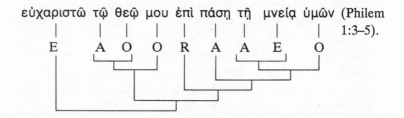

εὐχαριστῶ τῷ θεῷ μου ἐπὶ πάσῃ τῇ μνείᾳ ὑμῶν (Philem 1:3–5).

This may be rewritten as:

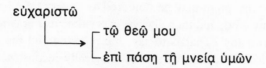

"I thank my God in all my remembrance of you" contains two event words εὐχαριστῶ and μνείᾳ. The second is related to the first by ἐπί signifying a *time* relationship. The term μνείᾳ has the same subject as εὐχαριστῶ, meaning essentially 'I thank when I remember'. The abstract πάσῃ points to the 'totality' of the event, this is, 'I always remember', with ὑμῶν as the object affected: 'I always remember you', that is, 'I think of you at all times'. The time relation involves that the meaning is: 'every time I think of you, I thank my God'. The construction following εὐχαριστῶ continues by linking a time abstract (πάντοτε) to εὐχαριστῶ amplifying ἐπὶ πάσῃ τῇ μνείᾳ ὑμῶν. The time designation points to a relationship with two events:

'I always thank when I pray ('make my prayer', ποιούμενος being an abstract of cause), and (I do it) with joy'. That is, 'I pray, and I am delighted'—an event of communication and an event of psychological experience. The term πάντοτε itself is amplified by a phrase ἐν πάσῃ δεήσει μου ὑπὲρ πάντων ὑμῶν in which ἐν is a relational localizing, so to speak, the πάντοτε phrase. Therefore ἐν takes up the time designation:

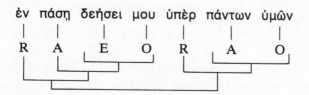

'Every time I pray for all of you' is therefore a longer phrase substituting for πάντοτε. This involves that the meaning of the whole sentence up to this point may be rendered as: 'every time I think of you, I thank my God, and then always, every time as I pray for all of you, I pray with joy'. That is to say, the *thinking* and the *praying* accompanies his expression of thanks. Logically reconstructed this would mean: 'every time I think of you, I pray for all of you thanking my God with great joy'.

But the construction following εὐχαριστῶ still continues with:

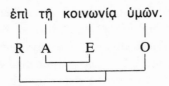

The ἐπί now introduces an event as the content of εὐχαριστῶ: 'I thank God for your partnership', that is, 'I thank God that you are participating, that you are sharing in my work'. The term κοινωνία is now linked to three things by three relational abstracts εἰς, ἀπό, and ἄχρι, of which the first signifies the goal, while the latter two are time restrictions specified by the abstracts τῆς πρώτης ἡμέρας and τοῦ νῦν. The term κοινωνία is an event word linked to εὐαγγέλιον by εἰς to indicate that the good news (itself an event) is the goal of their partnership, and that their participating (i.e., their help in spreading the good news) started right from the beginning and is continuing into the present. This may be schematized as:

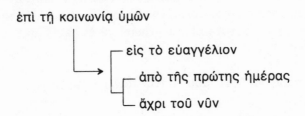

We may now join all the parts of the sentence together restructuring the semantic content based on the deep structure notions as represented in the surface structure. This may now be rendered as: 'every time I think of you, I pray for all of you. And when I pray I especially thank my God with joy for the fact that you shared with me in spreading the good news from the first day until now'. This reconstruction of the meaning of Philem 1:3–5 rendered the nominalized events by verbs in order to make the participants more explicit, and also to account for the emphasis εὐχαριστῶ carries as the matrix of the sentence by emphasizing the expression of thanks.

To appreciate the difference between a surface structure and a deep structure presentation of a text the above rendering may be compared with the translation of Philem 1:3-5 in the *RSV*, which is a literal translation representing the surface structure. The rendering given above is a dynamic translation of the text based on the deep structure relationships with an eye to the surface structure style in emphasizing particulars:

I thank my God in all my remembrance of you, always in every prayer of mine for you all making my prayer with joy, . . . thankful for your partnership in the gospel from the first day until now.	Every time I think of you, I pray for all of you. And when I pray I especially thank my God with joy for the fact that you shared with me in spreading the good news from the first day until now.

This passage did not require too many transformations, and so the translation which kept to the surface structure (*RSV*) is fairly comprehensible, despite certain obscurities. However, it is clear that when the surface structure makes it difficult to understand the utterance, only the deep structure can help. The more complex the passage, the more the need to analyze it in terms of its deep structure. For example, in Eph 1:5–7 the surface structure reads: ". . . having predestined us unto the adoption of children by Jesus Christ to himself, according to the good pleasure of his will, to the praise of the glory of his grace, wherein he hath made us accepted in the beloved in whom we have redemption through his blood, the forgiveness of sins, according to the riches of his grace" (*KJV*). A translation made according to the deep structure will be as follows: '. . . because God had already decided to make us his children through Jesus Christ. He did this because he wanted to and it gave him pleasure to do so. Let us praise the wonderful favor he gave us. This favor is that he gave us his Son, whom he loved. Yes, it is because Jesus died for us that God set us free. With this I mean that God forgives our sins. How abundant is the favor he showed us'.

Here are some of the transformations used in this translation:

(a) υἱοθεσία—'adoption': E = 'God makes us his children'.

(b) εὐδοκία—'good pleasure': E = 'God is glad about it'.

(c) εὐδοκία τοῦ θελήματος—'good pleasure of his will': E + E = 'God wants to do it and therefore he is glad about it', i.e., 'it gives him pleasure to do so'.

(d) εἰς ἔπαινον—'to the praise': R + E = 'it serves as praise' = 'that is why we must praise' = 'let us praise'.

(e) δόξα τῆς χάριτος—'glory of his grace': A + E = 'the favor he gives is wonderful' = 'the wonderful favor he gives'.

(f) ἀπολύτρωσις—'redemption': E = 'God redeems us' = 'God sets us free'.

(g) διὰ τοῦ αἵματος αὐτοῦ—'through his blood': R + E = 'because Christ died for us'.

(h) ἄφεσις τῶν παραπτωμάτων—'forgiveness of sins': E + E = 'God forgives us our sins/the sins we commit'.

(i) πλοῦτος τῆς χάριτος αὐτοῦ—'riches of his grace': A + E = 'he gives an abundant favor'.

The longer the units that are analyzed, the more complex the relations are between the different elements. The structure of these relations demonstrates how semantic information can stretch across word and even sentence boundaries. Therefore the analyses given above have not yet gone far enough. The moment a sentence boundary is crossed, it is absolutely necessary to consider the relations between sentences in a paragraph. These relations are important to determine the semantic groupings of sentences. In other words, just as a variety of relations exists within a sentence, so certain relations exist between sentences which provide the condition for the unity of the text argument. To determine the meaning of a passage we must consider the course of the argument. The entire discourse is an interwoven unit where the smallest group of sentences to be analyzed is the paragraph after which the relations between the paragraphs demonstrate the total argument. Semantics is concerned not only with words or even sentences, but also with the relations that permeate an entire argument. The analysis of this is at present called "discourse analysis" or "text analysis." The term "text analysis," though more compact than "discourse analysis," is usually avoided since it has certain associations with the text criticism in Greek studies and so could lead to confusion. The theory and practice of discourse analysis will be discussed in the next chapter.

Chapter 10

Semantics Is More Than
the Meaning of Sentences

Anyone who wants to say something is immediately confronted with a variety of possibilities that language offers him. This means that the same thing can be said in various ways. If a person is annoyed he can say, 'I don't appreciate it' or 'don't do that again' or 'stop it'. The selection made from the material of language is of cardinal importance, since every choice leads to different nuances. Moreover, if a large amount of material has to be communicated the arrangement assumes greater importance. Indeed, everyone who uses language in some way arranges what must be said. The so-called semantic performance of a person has been described in the following way by Hutchins (1971:204):

> From the precepts, concepts, etc. of the "cognitive experience" he wishes to communicate, a speaker selects those characteristics which are sufficient to specify his intended reference and which have counterparts in the semons of his language. Simultaneously these semons are organized as a semon network and those sememes are selected which can contain the semons and their specified interrelationships in an appropriate sememic formula.

Hutchins applies his idea to the structure of sentences, yet it is equally valid for larger sections of language. In written language it is of the utmost importance to arrange the material neatly. If the arrangement is too transparent then the communication becomes rigid, even monotonous. This is the reason why the structure of a well-written piece is not transparent. On the other hand, it is absolutely necessary that any communication should have structure, otherwise the piece would become incoherent. Abraham and Kiefer (1966) presented the following example to illustrate this point with reference to the arrangement of sentences: 'Yesterday Peter saw a film he had never seen before. The film was about a famous actress'. In this order the two sentences form one discourse. The second sentence enlarges upon the term 'film' in the first sentence by stating something about its content. If the sentences are reversed in order then no unity can be found between them—and therefore they would not constitute a discourse.

Different languages and different cultures have their own ways of communicating, and so the order in which the elements appear will differ. In Matt 2:1 the Greek order reads: "Jesus was born in Bethlehem in Judea during the reign of Herod. After his birth men who studied the stars from the East arrived in Jerusalem and inquired. . . ." The order in which the events are narrated follows the pattern of ancient Greek: the place is mentioned first and then the time. In a discourse such as this a language like Afrikaans would generally favor the reverse sequence: time, place. This would show the connection between the two sentences. If the Greek order is maintained an Afrikaans-speaking reader may feel that the first sentence is almost a preliminary announcement loosely attached to the discourse. The Greek order must be restructured to give: 'during the reign of Herod, Jesus was born in Bethlehem in Judea. At that time men who. . . . "

The narration of the death of John the Baptist in Mark 6 has an order in the Greek text that is heavily loaded with motivations. This means that the elements of the narrative are not produced merely in chronological order, but in terms of kernel issues which are continually motivated. Verse 17 is a typical example: "Herod himself sent for John, arrested him, had him chained and put in jail because of Herodias his brother Philip's wife whom he married." The motivation for putting John in jail is given as background information to highlight the issue that Herod put him in jail. The logical order of the events is: Herodias was the wife of Philip, Philip was the brother of Herod, Herod took his brother's wife, John criticized Herod, Herod had John arrested and put in jail. P. C. Stein (1974) discussed how the Greek order sounded very unnatural to a group of translation consultants in Nigeria. The connection between Herod's marriage to Herodias and the arrest of John the Baptist remained a mystery to them until the order of events was adjusted to fit the narrative style of Nigerians. Similarly, Deibler (1968) showed how Mark 6:17–20 consisted of twenty-four kernel statements whose chronological order was quite different from the order of the Greek text. In the Greek we find the event which chronologically occurred right at the beginning only mentioned when nearly halfway through the text.

A good illustration of the importance of discourse patterns can be found in Grimes and Glock (1970). They analyzed some of the typical orders of narrative in Saramacca, a language of the people of Surinam. One feature observed was that a repetitious phrase was always added between sentences when indicating the connection. For example: '. . . then he arrived at Mama Dam. With reference to his arrival at Mama Dam they loaded the boat until they were finished'. The final phrase is also of importance. If the sentence had ended with 'loaded the boat' a Saramaccan would wonder why the loading of the boat was never finished. Padućeva (1974) examined several construction patterns and claimed that the repetition of semantic elements is of great importance for most languages. He stated that "the coherence of a text within a paragraph is founded to a significant degree upon the repetition in adjacent phrases of the same semantic elements."

In the NT, Acts 1:1–5 can be used as an example. The Greek narrative must be transformed into the receptor language's narrative mode if the connection between events is to be comprehended. An English narrative would arrange the text as follows: verse 1, 2c, 3b, 3a, 4a, 2b, 4b, 5. To illustrate the difference the following two columns can be compared. The A column shows the Greek order, the B column the English.

A	B
In my first book, Theophilus, I wrote about all the things Jesus did and taught until the day he was taken up to heaven after he had given instructions through the Holy Spirit to his disciples whom he had chosen. After his death he showed himself to them	In my first book, Theophilus, I wrote about all the things Jesus did and taught until the day he was taken up to heaven. I wrote about his appearance to his disciples during forty days and his discussions with them about the Kingdom of God and also the

alive with many signs and appeared to them for forty days and talked about the Kingdom of God. When he was still with them he ordered them not to leave Jerusalem but to wait for the promise of the Father he told them about when he said: John baptized you with water, but soon you will be baptized by the Holy Spirit.

many signs he showed to prove that he was alive. Before he was taken up to heaven during one of the gatherings with his disciples he gave them orders through the Holy Spirit and said: Do not leave Jerusalem but wait for the gift of the Father I told you about when I said: John baptized you with water but you will soon be baptized with the Holy Spirit.

To understand any text it is necessary to know how the text was structured. From this analysis the contents can be rearranged, and then transformed into the narrative pattern of the receptor language. The analysis of any text unavoidably begins with the surface structure simply because this is the material the author (or speaker) offers to us. However, the author did not himself begin with the surface structure. The surface structure is rather the result of a process. The restructuring of the narrative is only one small part of the process since layers of deep structures exist. In this connection it is also helpful to bear in mind the actual process of communication. This process has been elaborated upon in Nida (1972).

In the present discussion the relations between deep and surface structures in the process of communication can be described as follows:

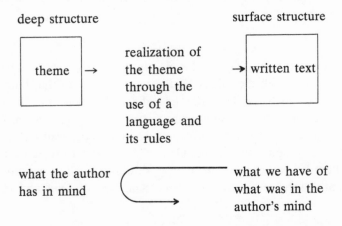

deep structure

theme → realization of the theme through the use of a language and its rules → written text

surface structure

what the author has in mind

what we have of what was in the author's mind

This diagram shows only *how* the author rendered his thoughts in the written text, but not *what* they were. From an analysis of the written text the theme must be recovered. A finer analysis than merely rearranging the narrative order must be done. The bent arrow of the diagram indicates that the recovering is not merely an elaboration of the surface structure in order to expose the deep structure. It is also a tracing of the path the author took in order to present his theme in a textual form. The text, therefore, has form as well as meaning. Since we are here concerned with written documents, this means that any text by nature has a particular form which may be called its overt or surface structure. The surface structure is, in the main, represented by the syntactic relationship between its constituents. This overt structure is, therefore, the form in which the semantic content which the author had in mind is expressed. The author, as it were, "moved" from the semantic content to the syntactic form. Our analysis must then, of necessity, move from the syntactic form to the semantic content.

The ultimate purpose of the type of analysis presented in this study is primarily semantic, and yet it is based upon so-called colon structure, which is generally regarded as essentially syntactic. In this analysis the term *colon* is used in a sense entirely different from what it normally means in English, for here *colon* parallels essentially what the ancient Greek grammarians spoke of as a kind of thought unit. However, in this analysis the colon is defined, not in terms of its semantic unity, but in terms of certain specific grammatical structures which in many ways parallel what would be regarded as sentences in English. But as will be made clearer in later sections, a colon is defined quite specifically in terms of syntactic structure.

The fact that the ultimate purpose of this analysis is semantic (that is, to determine the meaning of a passage or discourse) may create certain problems for some persons, unless they bear constantly in mind the fact that syntax and semantics cannot be neatly separated, for syntactic structures always carry meaning and meaning is not found apart from formal structures. But though syntax and semantics cannot be neatly isolated one from the other, their distinctive features must be clearly distinguished if one is to have a sound basis for determining the meaning of any text.

Discourse analysis based upon the use of colons is nothing more than a technique for mapping the form of a text in such a way that the syntactic relationships of the constituent parts can be most readily recognized. The syntactic relationships are crucial since they point most clearly to the semantic content. Thus by recognizing the colons as the first step in procedure, one can advance systematically to uncovering the meaningful units which may be said to "flow out of" or "emerge from" these syntactic structures. By analyzing not only the internal structure of individual colons, but also the relationships between colons, one can determine in a significant way the manner in which meaningful units cluster together and thus provide a satisfactory basis for a semantic interpretation of a text. But this means that one must always take into consideration both the surface structure of the syntax as well as the underlying deep structure with its crucial semantic elements.

It would, of course, be possible to begin an analysis with any one of the recognized language units such as morphemes, words, phrases, sentences, paragraphs, and so on. One may start with the smallest possible units which carry meaning and build up to the larger units, or one may do exactly the opposite, namely, begin with the larger units and analyze all the succeedingly more embedded or included units. It is also possible to begin with full sentences and work down into the internal structure of the sentence and work up to the paragraphs, sections, and even the entire discourse.

To analyze the thematic development of any utterance or discourse, it is, however, unwise to start with the smallest units, since the resulting segmentations or "cuts" in the discourse result in too many fragmentary items, and it is extremely difficult to put all of these together in an efficient and convincing manner. On the other hand, starting with the paragraph or even a larger section almost inevitably entails too big a chunk for effective analysis. Accordingly, from a practical point of view the colon (as here defined) seems to be in many respects the most feasible unit. The justification for this lies in the fact that it is the most closely linked complete construction. This means that syntactically the colon is the most easily identified unit and from the semantic standpoint it becomes one of the most useful units since it is essentially equivalent to a so-called proposition. Because the colon is the most closely linked complete construction, one can most readily determine its internal structure, and since the colon also consists of what may be regarded as a kind of proposition, it can be most readily and usefully linked to other colons to form important semantic groupings.

Though, as already mentioned, a colon as defined in this analysis is similar in many ways to a sentence, it is important not to confuse a colon with a sentence as a unit that begins with a capital letter and ends with a period or full stop. While the colon is defined clearly in terms of structural patterns in Greek, it may be useful at this point to illustrate some of the distinctive features of colons by means of corresponding English sentences. First of all, a colon consists normally of a subject and a predicate (though in Greek a subject may be included as a suffix on a verb). Any elements in the structure are directly dependent on or subordinate to either the head word of the subject or the head word of the predicate. This means, for example, that a sentence like 'my good friend almost always arrives late' would be regarded as a single colon consisting of a subject expression 'my good friend' and a predicate expression 'almost always arrives late'. The subject expression could, of course, be amplified by a relative clause, for example, 'my good friend who lives in France', and the predicate element could likewise be amplified by a dependent temporal clause such as 'when he has an appointment'. The element may consist of more than one part, for example, 'my good friend and his wife always arrive late'. Similarly, the predicate may consist of more than one element arranged in a coordinate manner, for example, 'my good friend came and gave me a book'. But when coordinate predications are combined by such so-called conjunctions as 'and', 'but', 'or', and 'for' (and similarly in Greek by δέ, καί, ἀλλά, and οὖν), one is no longer dealing with a single colon, but more than one colon. For example, the expression 'John sings and Mary writes' is regarded as a compound sentence in English, but in terms of colon analysis there would be two colons, one consisting of 'John sings' and the other of 'Mary writes'. One may argue that there is some kind of semantic connection between these two subject-predicate constructions, for no one would utter such a sentence without presuming some kind of link, however tenuous. But from the standpoint of the syntactic analysis, neither part is integrally or dependently related to the other. On the other hand, the sentence 'John sings while Mary writes' would be regarded as a single colon, since 'while Mary writes' is a temporal restriction imposed on 'sings' and is both syntactically and semantically dependent. A colon, therefore, is a unit of grammatical structure with clearly marked internal dependencies.

Though colons constitute the basic units employed in the analysis of a text, the semantic content of a total discourse cannot be determined by merely adding up the semantic content of each colon. The reason for this is that colons themselves cluster together in larger units, which in turn have their own distinctive semantic content and unity. The total discourse always entails a hierarchy of units in which, for example, there may be a number of major sections or chapters which consist of a series of paragraphs. These paragraphs may be regarded as colon clusters containing a series of individual colons, and these in turn are made up of clauses, phrases, and words. These units or divisions are the structural sections by which the total information is organized into recognizable groupings. In a sense continuous discourse, whether a speech act of a written document, is essentially a synthetic process, a kind of "putting together of units" which can only to a certain extent be considered separately, since these units actually communicate by means of a highly integrated and complex set of dependency relations.

Though the colon is the basic unit employed in discourse analysis, the most relevant unit for the explication of the semantic content of a discourse is the paragraph, since it is the largest unit possessing a single unitary semantic scope. The colon, however, is the most convenient starting point for the analysis of a text, since paragraphs are generally too large to handle from the outset. Though the colon is the most tightly structured syntactic unit, the paragraph is rhetorically more significantly structured than the colon, and since any text must be analyzed both from the standpoint of its syntactic as well as its rhetorical form, both the colons and the paragraphs are of fundamental importance.

It would be a mistake, however, to regard a paragraph as being necessarily that section of a discourse which in printed communication is marked by indentation or a similar convention. There is, of course, usually some relationship between indentation and the structural form of a paragraph, but the paragraph, in contrast to the colon, is essentially a cohesive unit in terms of its particular scope and topic. In fact, the paragraph is defined primarily in terms of its thematic unity, since it normally deals with only one concept (or aspect of an extended concept) or one aspect of an episode or object. This means that in general any total discourse that is longer than one paragraph must obviously be analyzed primarily in terms of the relationships between the constituent paragraphs.

The colon, as a basic unit of analysis, may consist of only a single word or, in some instances, of even a single sound which functions essentially like such a word. But such one-word colons function basically in the same way as colons consisting of two or more words, since one-word colons normally entail an ellipsis which can be supplied from the context. One-word colons (often spoken of as minor sentences in English, for example, 'please', 'ouch', 'yes') are not only relatively less frequent in occurrence, but obviously their analysis requires some kind of supplementation from other elements in the context. The structural relations within a colon become obvious as soon as one considers colons consisting of at least two words, but not merely two words chosen at random. The typical colon is a construction consisting of a nominal element (henceforth referred to as N) and a verbal element (henceforth noted as V). This means that utterances such as 'up there' or 'in the basket', though often occurring in conversation as isolated elements and therefore constituting minor sentence types (which depend upon contextual ellipsis), are by no means typical. A typical colon would be a combination such as 'John walks' or 'Nancy sleeps'. Such a combination of a subject and a predicate is the major characteristic of colons (and of sentences) in languages all over the world. The type of discourse analysis considered in this volume is based on the fact that the major colon types of a language can be derived from this simple structure of N + V.

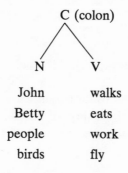

In a number of languages (including Greek, of course) a substitute for the nominal element (for example, pronouns such as 'I', 'you', 'we', 'he', 'she', 'they', 'it') may be combined with the verbal element to constitute a single word, but one which is semantically complex in the sense that it contains two elements which are not semantically dependent one upon the other. In Greek 'we walk' would be represented as βαδίζομεν, a single word but at the same time a colon which overtly displays the nominal element in the personal ending -μεν and the verbal element in the stem βαδιζ-.

We have already mentioned one important reason for speaking of colons in Greek rather than using the term "sentences." Since the word *sentence* would suggest to many readers any combination of clauses combined by means of so-called coordinate conjunctions such as 'and', 'or', 'but', 'for', and since Greek writers tended to combine almost all colons by means of some type of conjunction, it would mean that from a purely formal standpoint (based on analogies in present-day European languages) a sentence would be enormously long and involved. But there is still an additional reason for speaking of colons rather than sentences, for in certain linguistic analyses the term *sentence* (with the abbreviation S) has been employed in speaking of any syntactic string which may be less or even more than a colon. For example, some linguists would insist on analyzing the string 'the horse and the bull are grazing' as consisting of three S's:

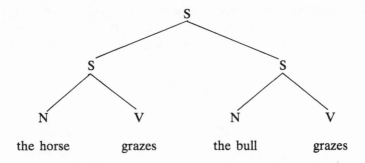

This type of diagram is rather confusing since it suggests that there are three sentence structures. In reality, of course, the expression 'the horse and the bull are grazing' seems to be far more satisfactorily analyzed as a single S:

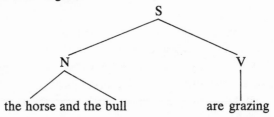

64871

The reason for adopting this second analysis is essentially the fact that without further information about the expression 'the horse and the bull are grazing', one would assume that there is some kind of joint activity or relationship involved in the horse and the bull, that is to say, they would likely be grazing at the same time and possibly even in the same field. From the standpoint of colon analysis, the expression 'the horse and the bull are grazing' would be regarded as a single colon. Some linguists, however, insist that every subject-predicate relationship is essentially an S, and therefore in a sentence such as 'Peter said that his dog is clever' the relationships would be diagrammed as follows:

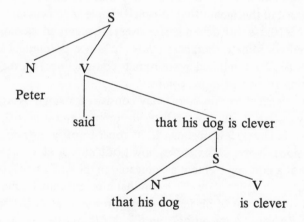

The string 'that his dog is clever' is a noun phrase complement containing the clause 'his dog is clever', but such a clause should not be regarded as a colon, for it is only a dependent part of a colon, that is to say, it is dependent upon the verb 'said' in the sense that it is the content of what is said. In the above diagram of 'Peter said that his dog is clever' the initial S would be equivalent to a colon, but the second S would only be a dependent subject-predicate structure.

Based upon the definition of a colon as used in this volume, in the sentence 'the man went to Boston and the boy played in his room' there would be two colons, since there is no direct dependency relationship between 'the man went to Boston' and 'the boy played in his room'. This English sentence is diagrammed by a number of linguists as:

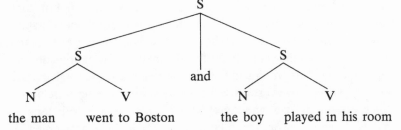

In this instance we would analyze 'the man went to Boston' as being one colon and 'the boy played in his room' as being the second colon. The conjunction 'and' would only be a transitional element between colons. All of this means that so-called simple sentences and complex sentences (those with dependent clauses) are regarded as colons, while so-called coordinate sentences (those in which potentially independent clauses are combined by coordinate conjunctions) are regarded as consisting of two or more colons.

In its shortest form a colon may consist of a single word, but as already noted, it will always have a nominal and a verbal element (unless, as in a few instances, it consists of a highly elliptical expression). Note, for example, how βαδίζει, νοσεῖ, and δίδωμι all consist of a nominal element as indicated in the suffix and a predicate element in the verb stem. The nominal element may be made more explicit by the use of an independent pronoun, as in the sentences οὗτος βαδίζει, αὕτη νοσεῖ, and ἐγὼ δίδωμι, in which case the nominal element is rhetorically emphatic. But the nominal element may also be a noun, noun phrase, or nominal clause as in οἱ ἵπποι βόσκονται or οἱ ταῦτα ποιήσαντες ἔφυγον, but the same principle of a colon consisting of nominal and verbal elements still applies:

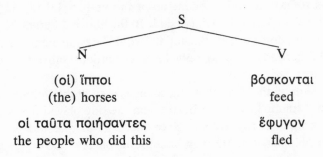

The nominal element may be extended as in ὁ ἵππος καὶ ὁ ταῦρος βόσκονται. This should generally, following our previous argumentation, not be analyzed as two separate sentences ὁ ἵππος βόσκεται and ὁ ταῦρος βόσκεται—and thus posed as two colons. A colon, being a construction unit conveying a coherent piece of information, will generally require ὁ ἵππος καὶ ὁ ταῦρος βόσκονται to be a single unit, that is, one colon. Yet, it stands to reason that a speaker may use the above mentioned string in such a way that by the particular intonation pattern employed to vocalize the string, one may tell that special emphasis is placed on the two participants of the action in order to communicate the information as 'the horse and the bull are grazing'. Such a vocalization of this string may be interpreted as 'the horse is grazing and besides this event, the bull is also grazing'. In this case the surface structure representation is not merely 'the horse and the bull are grazing' (that is to say one colon), but the **'and'** shows that the surface structure representation is equivalent to 'the horse is grazing and the bull is grazing' (that is to say, two colons). In written communication one may employ punctuation, italics, capitalization, or some other device to highlight this fact. Since in ancient literature such procedures were never used, examples as ὁ ἵππος καὶ ὁ ταῦρος βόσκονται may occasionally be regarded as ambiguous, since it is possible (though perhaps generally not probable) that a reader may understand such a string as 'the horse is grazing and the bull is also grazing'. We have to resort to the structure of the whole paragraph in which such a string appears, or to the word order—say chiasm or unusual position—to help us decide how to analyze the string. In Luke 21:10 (ἐγερθήσεται ἔθνος ἐπ' ἔθνος καὶ βασιλεία ἐπὶ βασιλείαν) one may argue that the initial position of ἐγερθήσεται involves emphasis, and that this string actually represents ἐγερθήσεται ἔθνος ἐπ' ἔθνος καὶ ἐγερθήσεται βασιλεία ἐπὶ βασιλείαν. This may be further endorsed by the following colon (Luke 21:11) σεισμοί τε μεγάλοι καὶ κατὰ τόπους λιμοὶ καὶ λοιμοὶ ἔσονται, presenting the N + V elements in a chiastic arrangement ἐγερθήσεται + nominals : nominals + ἔσονται. In this latter colon σεισμοί may be taken as a first unit, with λιμοὶ καὶ λοιμοί as a second unit, thus giving two colons. This may be based on the judgement that λιμοὶ καὶ λοιμοί is separated from σεισμοί by κατὰ τόπους, and also on the basis of the chiastic pattern having two items contrasted on each side, that is, ἔθνος + βασιλεία : σεισμοί + λιμοὶ καὶ λοιμοί. The λιμοὶ καὶ λοιμοί may then be justified as a lexical unit coming at the end of the pattern and doubled in itself for stylistic emphasis. Therefore, if emphasis is taken into account as a vital feature in the structure of the discourse, Luke 21:10–11 may be analyzed as four colons. On the other hand a reader of the paragraph Luke 21:7–19 may regard the feature of emphasis as not being structurally dominant. In such a case he would analyze Luke 21:10–11 into only two colons.

In Rom 4:10 the statement πῶς οὖν ἐλογίσθη; ἐν περιτομῇ ὄντι ἢ ἐν ἀκροβυστίᾳ; οὐκ ἐν περιτομῇ ἀλλ᾽ ἐν ἀκροβυστίᾳ offers an interesting case. Should this, for example, be analyzed as consisting of five colons, in which case ἐλογίσθη would need to be understood with each contrastive element, or is it more probable that there is essentially a three-fold division in which ἐλογίσθη must be understood with each alternative set?

    (a) πῶς οὖν ἐλογίσθη

    (b) ἐλογίσθη   ⌐ἐν περιτομῇ ὄντι
                      ⌊ἢ ἐν ἀκροβυστίᾳ

    (c) ἐλογίσθη   ⌐οὐκ ἐν περιτομῇ
                      ⌊ἀλλ᾽ ἐν ἀκροβυστίᾳ

It is essential to realize that in continuous discourse the multiple relationships are often highly complex and must often be stated in terms of multiple dimensions. It is therefore impossible to treat such structures as amenable to fixed sets of rules. Different alternatives must be considered on the basis of degrees of probability, and this is particularly true of stylistic features in which the subtle and often multidimensional factors make any rigid analysis quite impossible.

Since colon analysis is primarily a procedure dealing with continuous discourse, it must take into account all possible formal features, not only those involving syntax, but all stylistic features which may be regarded as being on a rhetorical level. One must begin with syntactic features, which in a sense have priority since they constitute ways in which basic relationships between fundamental units are most clearly marked. But the rhetorical features of style must also be considered when one is attempting to analyze the semantic content of any colon or paragraph or even larger unit.

In general, syntactic structures point to a single semantic solution, that is to say, most syntactic structures are not fundamentally ambiguous, but there are a number of syntactic features which permit of two or more possible analyses, and one must then try to determine which of the underlying alternative semantic structures is being reflected in the syntactic forms.

It would be wrong to think that one uses merely syntactic analysis up to a point when ambiguity occurs after which one must employ semantic analysis. In fact, all syntactic constructions have semantic implications, that is to say, they have syntactic meaning. But when a syntactic construction is ambiguous in meaning, then one must employ an analysis of the meaning which depends upon a wider framework than the specific syntax of an individual colon or sentence.

In Rom. 1:17 the expression ὁ δὲ δίκαιος ἐκ πίστεως ζήσεται may be analyzed in terms of two different sets of syntactic relations:

(1) 'the righteous shall live by faith' or
(2) 'he who is righteous by means of faith shall live'.

The purely syntactic arguments cannot resolve the ambiguity, and one can readily see why ἐκ πίστεως has been traditionally treated as in a dependent relationship to ζήσεται rather than to δίκαιος, since a phrase such as ἐκ πίστεως expressing means would normally be related to a verb such as ζήσεται rather than to an adjective such as δίκαιος. Unfortunately a reference to Hab 2:4 in the LXX or even to the Hebrew OT does not provide a satisfactory basis for analyzing this quotation, since it is a rather free quotation. But despite the tradition which tends to relate ἐκ πίστεως to the verb ζήσεται, there seems every reason to believe that in terms of the total discourse ἐκ πίστεως should be related to δίκαιος. This interpretation of ὁ δὲ δίκαιος ἐκ πίστεως ζήσεται on the basis of the wider context of the Epistle to the Romans is further confirmed by the implication that δίκαιος involves not some abstract characteristic of a person, but a state of being resulting from an activity. If, for example, δίκαιος is understood as referring to a person who has been put right with God, then quite clearly ἐκ πίστεως seems to be a fully justified attributive.

Actual ambiguities do not have a high frequency of occurrence, but it is true that within the narrow scope of an individual phrase, clause, or even colon, there may be frequent instances of potential ambiguities, most of which, however, are resolved by the wider context.

As already noted, the Greek word κῶλον was used by ancient Greek grammarians and stylists to designate a stretch of language having an interrelated grammatical construction and expressing a coherent thought. It is not used here in precisely the same way as the ancient grammarians used κῶλον (see, for example, Demetrius περὶ ἑρμενείας), for they based their divisions into colons on logical units entailing numerous variations which would allow readers to analyze the structure of any paragraph in quite different ways. In contrast, therefore, to colon analysis as practiced by the Greeks and others in terms of so-called thought units, the term colon is used in this analysis in a rather precise way and refers to a unit of syntactic cohesion.

Though a colon is essentially a formal unit, nevertheless one may look upon it from a semantic point of view as consisting of a relatively coherent piece of information, that is to say, it is essentially a kind of proposition. Both semantically and syntactically, therefore, the colon is a single integrated structure. It always has either overtly or covertly a central matrix consisting of a subject and predicate, each having the possibility of extended features. This matrix consists of verbal forms and each syntactic relationship of these forms has a meaning. Furthermore, the unit as a whole has a meaning in the sense that it consists of a proposition. A colon, therefore, may be defined as *a structural unit having a particular syntactic form and a related semantic content*. Inevitably the semantic interpretation of a colon depends in considerable degree upon the syntactic relationships of the units within the colon. This does not rule out the fact that the semantic interpretation of a colon also depends upon the wider context in which the colon itself is embedded.

Since the meaning of any colon depends not only upon its internal relations, but also upon its external relations, one might want to develop a methodology in which one would attempt to look at both sets of relations at the same time. But such a procedure becomes exceedingly complex. From the standpoint of a more satisfactory methodology, it seems better to begin with the internal structure and its related meanings and then to move on to the analysis of the external relations and their meanings. This order of procedure seems to be justified in view of the fact that a high percentage of the meanings of a colon can be determined on the basis of the internal structure, and only in relatively fewer cases must one look to the external relations for the analysis of the meaning.

To summarize, one may say that the colon is the basic structural unit of a discourse having both form and meaning. Its form consists essentially in its syntactic patterning, while its meaning, consisting of the meanings of its lexical units and the structural relationships between the constituent parts, provides the fundamental data by which eventually the total semantic content of a discourse may be determined.

As already noted, a colon is a structural unit consisting of a nominal element and a verbal element, both of which may be expanded by coordinate series or by attributives which are syntactically dependent upon the so-called head words:

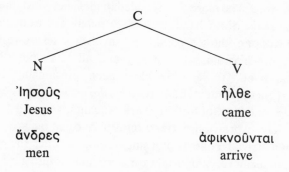

The nominal element can be expanded by coordinate additions:

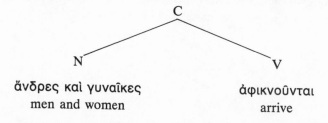

The nominal element may also be expanded by adding attributives, for example, deictic, quantitative, qualitative, etc.:

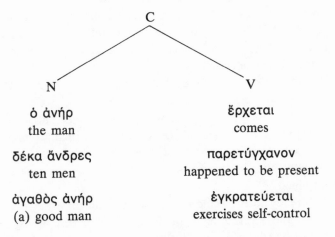

C	
N	V
ὁ ἀνήρ	ἔρχεται
the man	comes
δέκα ἄνδρες	παρετύγχανον
ten men	happened to be present
ἀγαθὸς ἀνήρ	ἐγκρατεύεται
(a) good man	exercises self-control

Although attributives which are added to a nominal element supply additional information, they do in fact restrict the range of reference of the head word. The more that is added to the head word, the more the potential range of the head word is restricted. For example οἱ δέκα ἀγαθοὶ ἄνδρες 'the ten good men' involves a severe restriction of ἄνδρες which could refer to any and all men, but οἱ specifies particular men, those who have been presumably mentioned previously in the context; δέκα restricts the meaning of ἄνδρες to ten such men, and ἀγαθοί further restricts qualitatively to a certain class of men. The expression οἱ δέκα ἀγαθοὶ ἄνδρες ἀφίκοντο 'the ten good men arrived' consists of a single colon in which the restrictions are semantically very important for a continuous discourse, since the attributives οἱ, δέκα, and ἀγαθοί all increase considerably what might be regarded as the specificity of ἄνδρες.

Attributives themselves may also be expanded by adding coordinate elements or by employing modifying clauses:

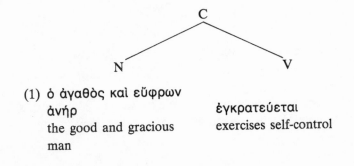

C	
N	V
(1) ὁ ἀγαθὸς καὶ εὔφρων ἀνήρ	ἐγκρατεύεται
the good and gracious man	exercises self-control

(2) ὁ ἀνὴρ ὅς ταῦτα
    ἐποίησε   παρατυγχάνεται
    the man who did this   happens to be present

The phrase ὅς ταῦτα ἐποίησε (or a corresponding participial phrase such as ταῦτα ποιήσας) has essentially the same function as ἀγαθός has in the expression ὁ ἀγαθὸς ἀνήρ. Similarly εὔφρων adds an additional qualifying feature and in colon analysis one would normally rewrite ὁ ἀγαθὸς καὶ εὔφρων ἀνήρ as:

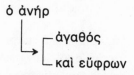

This type of graphic representation is merely a heuristic device to highlight the constituent elements of a phrase, but one may also rewrite ὁ ἀγαθὸς καὶ εὔφρων ἀνήρ as:

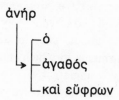

Both of the above notations clearly show that ἀνήρ in the expression ὁ ἀγαθὸς καὶ εὔφρων ἀνήρ has three attributives which restrict its range of reference, but the second diagram shows the relation of the three attributives in a more explicit manner. Nevertheless, the former method of diagramming is more generally employed, since it saves space, a factor which is particularly important in mapping a whole paragraph on a single page.

In the above examples a singular verbal element has been used throughout, but one can, of course, enlarge the verbal element by adding restrictions or by producing a coordinate series. *As long as all additions can be linked to a basic nominal element and a basic verbal element, the resulting structure consists of one colon.*

The coordinate series of a verbal element may at times seem to pose a problem of ambiguity. For instance, in the statement ὁ ἀνὴρ ἀπεκρίθη καὶ εἶπε . . . , some persons might want to assume that there are two colons because there are two verbs, but in reality ἀπεκρίθη καὶ εἶπε refers to a single activity even as ἀποκριθεὶς εἶπε would refer to a single activity. One can best diagram these relationships as:

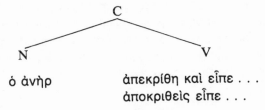

One may justify combining ἀπεκρίθη and εἶπε as being a coordinate series in the predicate of a single colon by pointing out that their meanings are very close together in semantic space and thus can be regarded as being merely two verbal means of referring to essentially the same activity. Justification for this analysis can also be based upon the fact that this doubling of expressions for saying reflects a Semitic usage. In Rom 1:25 the two verbal expressions ἐσεβάσθησαν καὶ ἐλάτρευσαν "they worshiped and served" may be regarded as complementary ways of speaking about religious devotion, and therefore may be interpreted as being means by which one may refer to closely related phases of essentially a single act.

The predicate element of any colon may involve a number of so-called expansions of the verbal element. These may consist of so-called direct objects, indirect objects, expressions of time, place, circumstances, purpose, result, and so forth. The following constitute three of the more frequently occurring structural types:

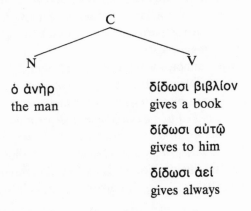

In the example δίδωσι βιβλίον, the term βιβλίον qualifies δίδωσι by identifying the object involved in the process of giving. In a sense βιβλίον restricts the giving to a particular type of object. It would be possible to expand this type of so-called direct object by a coordinate series, for example, δίδωσι βιβλίον καὶ κάλαμον 'he gives a book and a pen'. One may also substitute a clause having essentially the same syntactic function, for example, δώσουσιν ὃ ἐὰν αἰτήσηται 'they will give whatever he may ask'.

In the expression ὁ ἀνὴρ δίδωσι αὐτῷ the event δίδωσι is qualified by indicating who is indirectly involved in or affected by the event of giving. One may likewise have in this structural position a coordinate series, for example, δίδωσι αὐτῷ καὶ ταῖς γυναιξί 'he gives to him and to the women'. One may also substitute a dependent subject-predicate structure, for example δίδόασι τοῖς σὺν αὐτῷ οὖσιν 'they give to those who are with him'.

In the expression δίδωσι ἀεί the qualifying element ἀεί characterizes the event in terms of a temporal feature, but one may also employ a statement such as δίδωσι ἱλαρῶς 'he gives cheerfully', in which case ἱλαρῶς qualifies the manner of giving. Many other types of qualifications may be employed, for example, setting, reason, result, purpose, condition, concession, and the like. Nevertheless, as qualifications of the verb they function in a way basically similar to ἀεί and ἱλαρῶς. Furthermore, these qualifying elements may be added one to another, for example, δίδωσι ἀεὶ ἱλαρῶς 'he always gives cheerfully'.

As in the case of elements added to the nominal part of a colon, those expressions which are added to the verbal element also restrict the range of reference even as they supply further information. In other words, they add to the information, but they restrict the range of the head word or phrase. That means that the more that is added, the more the range of the head word or expression is restricted. Note, for example, the series of restrictions occurring in ὁ ἀγαθὸς ἀνὴρ ὅς ταῦτα ἐποίησε ἀεὶ πολὺ δίδωσι ἵνα σωθῆτε which may be diagrammed as follows.

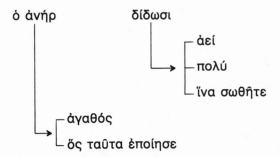

In the expression ὁ ἀγαθὸς ἀνὴρ ὃς ταῦτα ἐποίησε ἀεὶ πολύ δίδωσι ἵνα σωθῆτε, there is, however, a potential ambiguity, for certainly ἀεί may be related to ἐποίησε as well as to δίδωσι, though one would expect that if ἀεί were to qualify ἐποίησε, it would immediately precede ἐποίησε rather than follow.

The evidence that this sentence consists of a single colon is based upon the fact that each one of the elements is linked in one way or another to either the subject or the predicate elements.

One may also state the principal semantic relations involved in the graphic representation of the above sentence:

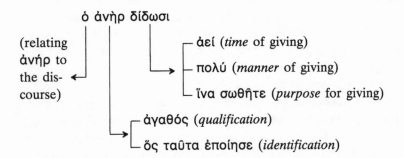

As may be clearly seen, the colon is a structure consisting of a nominal element and a verbal element which constitute the matrix of the colon, and both of these elements may be expanded by certain semantic restrictions, as long as these restrictions are linked directly to the basic elements of the matrix. There is no theoretical limit to the length of a colon. What is important is the structural relations involved in the constituent parts.

Finally, there is an additional type of expansion whereby a colon may be extended by means of an emotive element which may have a double function. In the first place, it may prompt attention, but it may also serve to characterize the colon as a whole rather than to qualify either the subject or the predicate elements. The addition of φεῦ 'alas' to a statement provides a kind of modal qualification for the statement itself, and the particle ναί 'yes, indeed' is likewise essentially modal in its semantic bearing on the colon with which it is combined. On the other hand, the addition of vocative expressions such as ἀδελφοί 'brothers' and ἄνδρες Ἰουδαῖοι 'fellow Jews' are perhaps better analyzed as being so-called minor sentence types, and thus in a sense consisting of a kind of colon with implied elliptical elements. For example, ἄνδρες Ἰουδαῖοι may be interpreted as simply 'you are fellow Jews'. On the other hand, in a statement such as ἀδελφοί, ἐγὼ λέγω ταῦτα ὑμῖν 'brothers, I say these things to you', one could analyze ἀδελφοί as being a qualification of or in apposition to ὑμῖν in a sense of 'you brothers' or 'you who are brothers'.

In summary, one may therefore list the following colons as representing the typical structures:

(1) ὁ ἀνὴρ δίδωσι
(2) ὁ ἀγαθὸς ἀνὴρ δίδωσι
(3) ὁ ἀνὴρ δίδωσι βιβλίον
(4) ὁ ἀνὴρ δίδωσι αὐτῷ
(5) ὁ ἀνὴρ δίδωσι ἀεί
(6) φεῦ ὁ ἀνὴρ δίδωσι

A colon, then, may be regarded as syntactically an expression having a matrix consisting of a nominal element and a verbal element along with such additions as are linked directly to either of the two elements of the matrix or additions which are in turn linked to other additions.

As long as a series of words is directly or indirectly related to a single matrix consisting of a nominal and verbal element, such an expression consists of a single colon. In the case of ὁ ἀνὴρ δίδωσι τοῖς ἀγαθὰ αἰτοῦσιν 'the man gives to those asking good things', τοῖς ἀγαθὰ αἰτοῦσιν is an indirect object of δίδωσι, while ἀγαθά is at the same time the direct object of αἰτοῦσιν. Similarly, in Rom 6:4, συνετάφημεν οὖν αὐτῷ διὰ τοῦ βαπτίσματος εἰς τὸν θάνατον, ἵνα ὥσπερ ἠγέρθη Χριστὸς ἐκ νεκρῶν διὰ τῆς δόξης τοῦ πατρός, οὕτως καὶ ἡμεῖς ἐν καινότητι ζωῆς περιπατήσωμεν constitutes a single colon with συνετάφημεν as its matrix consisting of both a verb and nominal element (the nominal element is in the suffix -μεν), but in Rom 6:13, μηδὲ παριστάνετε τὰ μέλη ὑμῶν ὅπλα ἀδικίας τῇ ἁμαρτίᾳ, ἀλλὰ παραστήσατε ἑαυτοὺς τῷ θεῷ ὡσεὶ ἐκ νεκρῶν ζῶντας καὶ τὰ μέλη ὑμῶν ὅπλα δικαιοσύνης τῷ θεῷ, there are two colons, since there are two matrices, παριστάνετε and παραστήσατε. Clearly, παραστήσατε cannot be analyzed as merely an addition to any one of the elements already dependent or added to παριστάνετε. Accordingly, παραστήσατε becomes the head word of the second colon.

When one is in doubt as to whether a particular element or expression is part of a colon or constitutes a colon in and of itself, one should immediately determine whether such an expression is syntactically linked to one and only one of the two elements in the subject-predicate matrix, that is to say, the nominal element or the verbal element or to any one of the additions which is already linked to the matrix. That is to say, the linking may be either direct or indirect.

In view of the structural linking of elements which constitute a colon, one may regard the colon as essentially a 'thought unit', but it would be wrong to regard any and every 'thought unit' as being a colon. Accordingly, one cannot use mere semantic features for marking off colons, since colons are basically syntactic structures by which a speaker or writer expresses propositions. For example, in Rom 1:11, ἐπιποθῶ γὰρ ἰδεῖν ὑμᾶς, ἵνα τι μεταδῶ χάρισμα ὑμῖν πνευματικὸν, the phrase ἵνα . . . πνευματικὸν is syntactically linked to ἐπιποθῶ . . . ὑμᾶς as an expression of purpose. The author could have certainly conveyed his thought as ἐπιποθῶ γὰρ ἰδεῖν ὑμᾶς αἰτία δὲ ἐστιν ἵνα μεταδῶ χάρισμα ὑμῖν πνευματικόν. In the latter case αἰτία . . . πνευματικόν is also an expression of purpose linked *semantically* with ἐπιποθῶ . . . ὑμᾶς, but it is not linked *syntactically* to ἐπιποθῶ . . . ὑμᾶς except by means of the conjunctive particle δέ, which marks coordinate relationships between colons rather than dependent relationships within a colon. In the first structure consisting of one colon, the purpose is expressed in a syntactically dependent manner. In the second structure, a relatively similar meaning is communicated, but the purpose is not syntactically dependent upon the expression ἐπιποθῶ . . . ὑμᾶς, and for that reason the second structure constitutes two colons.

In a continuous discourse it is important to maintain a clear distinction between the syntactic structure and the semantic relationships; and in order to establish a firm basis for semantic analysis, it is important to begin with the overt syntactic structure. Otherwise, one may engage in all types of fanciful intuitive judgments. Since the surface structure shows clearly how an author chose to present his message, it is this surface representation which is fundamental to a valid semantic interpretation.

In Rom 1:11 the conjunction γάρ in ἐπιποθῶ γὰρ . . . πνευματι-κὸν is a typical syntactic marker which relates ἐπιποθῶ . . . πνευ-ματικὸν to the previous statement in Rom 1:9–10. Though ἐπιποθῶ . . . πνευματικὸν is syntactically linked to the previous statement, it is not a dependent restriction upon any particular structure in the previous statement. It is rather a reason for the statement as a whole, and therefore not embedded within a part of it. As such, it stands as a separate colon in relationship to Rom 1:9–10 which is itself also a single colon. The fact that the clause in which γάρ occurs does not qualify any particular structure in the previous colon but rather semantically qualifies the entire content of the colon also means that γάρ is not a conjunction introducing a dependent clause, but rather a kind of transitional particle introducing a new colon.

A similar situation occurs in Matt 8:14–17 in which the clause ὅπως . . . ἐβάστασεν begins a new colon, since the sentence introduced by ὅπως is a conclusion to several preceding colons and is not directly dependent upon the immediately preceding expression πάντας . . . ἐθεράπευσεν. Accordingly, ὅπως serves not as a conjunction to mark the embedding of a dependent clause, but as a transitional particle marking the beginning of a separate colon.

In Matt 8:20 the statement λέγει αὐτῷ ὁ Ἰησοῦς, Αἱ ἀλώπεκες φωλεοὺς ἔχουσιν καὶ τὰ πετεινὰ τοῦ οὐρανοῦ κατασκηνώσεις, ὁ δὲ υἱὸς τοῦ ἀνθρώπου οὐκ ἔχει ποῦ τὴν κεφαλὴν κλίνῃ "Jesus said to him, The foxes have holes and the birds of the sky have nests, but the Son of Man does not have a place where he may lay his head" must be analyzed from two different perspectives. If one considers the entire statement λέγει . . . κλίνῃ, then obviously there is only one colon, since the quoted statement αἱ ἀλώπεκες . . . κλίνῃ is the so-called direct object of content of the verb λέγει. At the same time, the direct discourse, αἱ ἀλώπεκες . . . κλίνη consists of three colons, each with a separate subject and predicate expression. In all cases of embedded direct discourse it is essential to analyze the structures from two quite distinct viewpoints:

(1) the total expression introduced by some verb of speaking or writing; and

(2) the embedded elements which constitute a direct discourse.

All direct discourse constitutes in itself a discourse unit which is subject to the same principles of analysis as those employed in analyzing any type of discourse.

It is, of course, possible to treat the three embedded colons in Matt 8:20 as being subcolons, in other words, consisting of structures which function in a manner similar to colons as far as their interrelations are concerned, but are part of a larger colon in terms of the frame in which they occur.

Though the emphasis in this analysis is first of all on single colons, it would be wrong to think of discourses merely in terms of a series of more or less isolated colons, for colons always cluster together to form larger thematic units. These thematic units normally constitute a paragraph, and a series of thematic units consisting of paragraphs frequently combine to form a section or chapter of a discourse. But as already noted, from the standpoint of the thematic development of a discourse, the paragraph is a more fundamental unit than the colon itself. This approach parallels the statement made by Jordan (1965: 121) that a paragraph is a readily perceptible whole by which an author says "this much of my thought I wish you to consider separately from the rest because it seems to me to have a particular unity and to advance the idea in a peculiar way."

Though a paragraph is often treated in terms of being essentially a thematic or semantic unit, it nevertheless is often marked in a formal way, for example, by transitional particles, repeated words, parallel or chiastic structures, or introductory and/or terminal statements. The paragraph, as a series of semantically related colons, may have several different types of structures. For example, a paragraph may begin by a so-called paragraph sentence which states the theme of the paragraph, and what follows is simply an explication of that theme. On the other hand, it is possible to have a paragraph which develops various aspects of a theme and then presents the theme as a summary statement at the end of the paragraph. It is also possible for a paragraph to begin and end with a type of summary statement; or the middle of the paragraph may be the focal element, and the development may be towards that central position and then move away from it. The various patterns of structure may be illustrated graphically by the following diagrams:

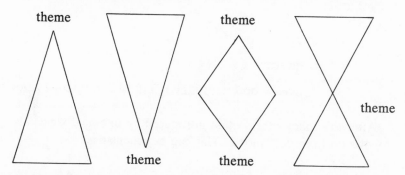

What is important is not so much the type of structural pattern of a paragraph, but rather the extent of its internal semantic unity in contrast with preceding and following thematic units or paragraphs.

A paragraph is then a type of formal-semantic structure consisting normally of a series of colons employed by the author to build up a larger semantic unit. The individual colons normally consist of coherent pieces of information (that is to say, propositions) which form semantic units in and of themselves, but which also contribute to the larger semantic structure of the paragraph. But if one is to do full justice to any discourse, it is essential to begin with the overt structures of the colons and to work towards the larger units of the discourse.

The following series of examples will illustrate this theoretical approach:

Example 1: Philemon 4–7

The first step when analyzing a segment of language is to mark out the construction units. Philem 4–7 appears in the *UBSGNT* text as one single sentence. The first aim of a discourse analysis is to divide the sentence into colon units. As was said earlier, the colons are nothing other than the thought units of the total expression. If, for example, five colons are found within a paragraph, then these five cooperate to form the whole expression by stating five major units of thought in relation to each other in a definite semantically determined pattern.

In the analysis of Philem 4–7 the following construction is found: the sentence begins with εὐχαριστῶ τῷ θεῷ μου πάντοτε followed by a participial construction μνείαν σου ποιούμενος ἐπὶ τῶν προσευχῶν μου. Two adverbial constructions can be linked to εὐχαριστῶ:

εὐχαριστῶ
    ┌─ πάντοτε
    └─ μνείαν σοῦ ποιούμενος ἐπὶ τῶν προσευχῶν μου

After this follows the section introduced by ἀκούων, which also follows on from εὐχαριστῶ. This can be schematized as:

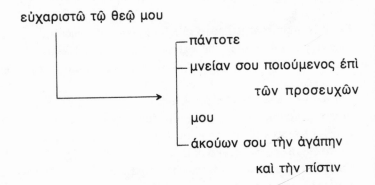

εὐχαριστῶ τῷ θεῷ μου
    ┌─ πάντοτε
    ├─ μνείαν σου ποιούμενος ἐπὶ
            τῶν προσευχῶν
         μου
    └─ ἀκούων σου τὴν ἀγάπην
            καὶ τὴν πίστιν

The relative sentence ἣν ἔχεις πρὸς τὸν κύριον Ἰησοῦν καὶ εἰς πάντας τοὺς ἁγίους that follows acts as an extension of ἀγάπην καὶ πίστιν. The part of the sentence beginning with ὅπως follows, but this cannot, naturally, succeed ἣν ἔχεις, εὐχαριστῶ, μνείαν σου ποιούμενος or ἀκούων. Among these ἣν ἔχεις and ἀκούων are excluded because it would not make any sense for the phrase to follow on from either of them. The other two are also unlikely antecedents for ὅπως, since the meaning would then be rather forced. It seems best to join ὅπως and what follows to an assumed προσεύχομαι based on a transformation of ἐπὶ τῶν προσευχῶν μου. The construction can then be explained as follows. Because πάντοτε is closely related to μνείαν . . . προσευχῶν μου the relations between the parts may be shown as: πάντοτε presents a fixing of the time of μνείαν . . . προσευχῶν μου, and together they fix the time of εὐχαριστῶ. The following section of the sentence (ἀκούων . . . πίστιν) presents the reason for εὐχαριστῶ. All this results in one sentence that begins with εὐχαριστῶ up to τοὺς ἁγίους at the end of verse 5. From ὅπως onwards we have a new construction built upon προσεύχομαι. This construction introduces a new colon. The γάρ at the beginning of verse 7 does not directly follow as an extension to any particular section of the two colons but rather introduces what has traditionally been described as a coordinate main clause. In more modern terminology the γάρ introduces a new colon that combines additively with the entire preceding colon. The γάρ, therefore, equals γ᾽ ἄρα. It is a transitional particle introducing a new colon, and not a conjunction introducing a dependant clause (see p. 114 above). Philem 4–7 can now be schematized on the basis of its colon structure (which is its syntactic structure) into three thought units that cover the four verses of the traditional text of Philemon:

1. εὐχαριστῶ τῷ θεῷ μου

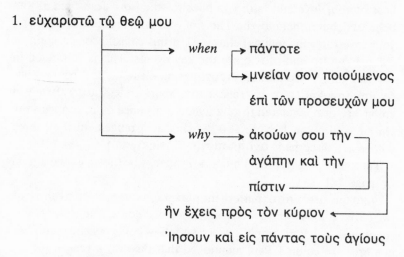

    when → πάντοτε

           → μνείαν σον ποιούμενος

           ἐπὶ τῶν προσευχῶν μου

    why → ἀκούων σου τὴν

           ἀγάπην καὶ τὴν

           πίστιν

     ἣν ἔχεις πρὸς τὸν κύριον ←

     Ἰησουν καὶ εἰς πάντας τοὺς ἁγίους

2. προσεύχομαι ὅπως . . . εἰς Χριστόν

3. χαρὰν γὰρ ἔσχον . . . ἀδελφέ

Before colons 2 and 3 are examined, colon 1 needs to be analyzed in further detail. The reason why Paul tells Philemon that he thanks God every time he prays, is given in two parts: ἀγάπην and πίστιν. The relative clause which follows also consists of two parts: τὸν κύριον Ἰησοῦν and πάντας τοὺς ἁγίους. It is understandable that Paul ties in love and faith with Jesus, but only love fits with the ἅγιοι—the fellow believers. Faith in Jesus and faith in cobelievers do not exist on the same level. However, this problem is solved when it is observed that the four elements are put in a chiastic arrangement. The chiasmus (with a basic pattern of a-b-b-a) is a popular form of style that is found in the NT. This results in the following:

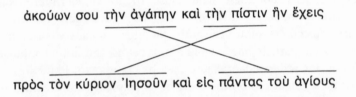

The chiasmus demonstrates how the text cannot be translated as 'I hear of your love and faith you have for the Lord Jesus and all the believers', but rather must be 'I hear of your faith in the Lord Jesus and your love for your fellow believers'. In this chiastic construction of colon 1 ἀγάπη and πίστις are the key events. This is continued in colons 2 and 3. Colon 2 has πίστις as an element, and colon 3 has ἀγάπη. In colon 2 πίστις is related to the phrase εἰς Χριστόν, while in colon 3 ἀγάπη is related to τῶν ἁγίων. This once more confirms the chiasmus of colon 1. Note also the chiastic arrangement if all three colons are discerned: ἀγάπη-πίστις-πίστις-ἀγάπη.

The entire paragraph of Philem 4–7 can now be shown as in diagram on page 121.

From this structure or pattern the paragraph can be seen to consist of two parts: colons 2 and 3 are an extension of colon 1. The entire text is concerned with Philemon's love for his fellow believers and their faith in Christ. In colon 1 Paul mentioned that this was a reason for his thankfulness to God. In colon 2 he continues with the fact that he prays for Philemon's faith to remain in action. The result of this faith is the observance of blessings which leads to Philemon's helpfulness to his

1. εὐχαριστῶ τῷ θεῷ μου

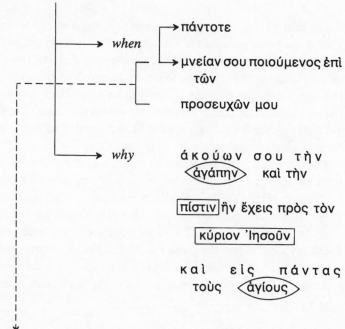

when → πάντοτε

→ μνείαν σου ποιούμενος ἐπὶ τῶν

προσευχῶν μου

why   ἀκούων σου τὴν ⟨ἀγάπην⟩ καὶ τὴν

[πίστιν] ἣν ἔχεις πρὸς τὸν

[κύριον Ἰησοῦν]

καὶ εἰς πάντας τοὺς ⟨ἁγίους⟩

2. προσεύχομαι ὅπως ἡ κοινωνία τῆς [πίστεώς] σου

ἐνεργὴς γένηται

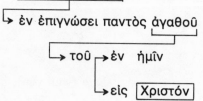

→ ἐν ἐπιγνώσει παντὸς ἀγαθοῦ

→ τοῦ → ἐν ἡμῖν

→ εἰς [Χριστόν]

3. χάραν γὰρ πολλὴν ἔσχον καὶ παράκλησιν ἐπὶ

τῇ ⟨ἀγάπῃ⟩ σου

→ ὅτι τὰ σπλάγχνα τῶν ⟨ἁγίων⟩ ἀναπέπαυται

διὰ σοῦ, ἀδελφέ

fellow believers (colon 3). Paul is glad about this, and he gives thanks to God.

The central idea of the entire argument is Philemon's love and faith. This is the *pivot point* of the paragraph. Each paragraph will have a pivot point. Sometimes one colon can take such a central position with respect to the other colons so that they all revolve, as it were, around this one colon. An example of this will be given later. In Philem 4–7 the focus is situated in the chiasmus. However, there is no fixed rule for determining the focus since it must be determined *ad hoc* every time from the pattern or structure of the paragraph.

The next step is to analyze the elements of the colons in terms of their kernel sentences. From this the following nuclear structures can be derived: 'I thank my God'—'I always pray'—'I call your name'—'I pray'. The relations between these kernel elements are as follows: 'I pray and mention you' = 'I pray for you; and every time I do this, I thank my God'. Then the reason, analyzed above, follows: 'because I hear of your faith in the Lord Jesus and of your love for your fellow believers'. Then follows colon 2 containing a difficult formulation which can be analyzed as:

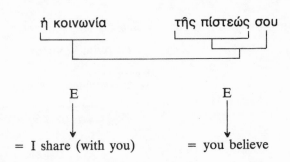

In this structure we have two event words in a genitive construction which can be transformed as: 'You believe and I share in your faith'. That is to say: 'you and I share in the faith'. Paul then continues by expressing the wish that this faith they share should be ἐνεργής, that is, that it should be active, diligent ἐν ἐπιγνώσει παντὸς ἀγαθοῦ 'in the knowledge of every good deed'. The word ἐπίγνωσις is an event word: 'we know'. So colon 2 means: 'I pray that the faith we share will bring us knowledge of all good things'. That is, that we know all the good things. These good things are ours (ἐν ἡμῖν) and have Christ as goal (εἰς Χριστόν). These are the things related to our faith. The other side of the coin relates to our love towards one another. This is stated in colon 3 which can be seen as:

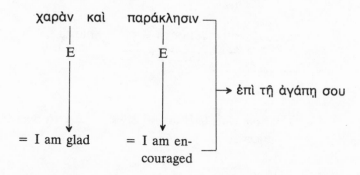

In other words, your love brings me a lot of joy and courage. The ὅτι phrase gives the reason for this with the idiomatic expression τὰ σπλάγχνα ἀναπέπαυται, literally, 'inner feelings are relieved'. This idiom can be transformed into 'help someone so that he can be glad'. That is, to gladden someone by helping him.

Using the above analysis and transformations, the entire text can be reconstructed by the following dynamic translation: 'Philemon, every time I pray I thank my God for you for I heard of your faith in the Lord Jesus and your love for your fellow believers. And I pray that the faith we share will make us to know the good things that are for us in view of Christ. Your faith my brother, brought me great joy and encouragement because you cheered up your fellow believers with the help you gave them'.

Example 2: Colossians 3:1–4

To analyze this text one will begin by marking out the construction units. The first is from εἰ οὖν συνηγέρθητε up to τοῦ θεοῦ καθήμενος. This section has a form analogous to a sentence such as 'I always give a book' that has been extended to 'I always give an interesting book'. Instead of 'I give' there is in Col 3:1 ζητεῖτε. Instead of 'book' τὰ ἄνω has been extended like 'interesting book' to οὗ ὁ Χριστός ἐστιν ἐν δεξιᾷ τοῦ θεοῦ καθήμενος. Instead of 'always' there is εἰ οὖν συνηγέρθητε τῷ Χριστῷ. In other words we find only one construction and so only one colon. However, this colon consists of smaller construction units that are tied to each other by the nuclear units as follows:

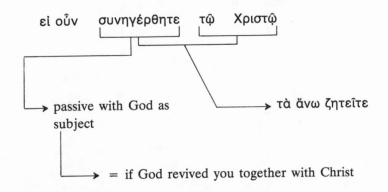

The relation between the sections εἰ . . . Χριστῷ and τὰ ἄνω ζητεῖτε is grammatically described as a conditional construction, but semantically the first is the motivation for the second. Therefore, the meaning can be formulated as: God revived you with Christ, so set your hearts on the things above (= in heaven). The term ἄνω is defined as οὗ ὁ Χριστός ἐστιν which is further qualified by ἐν δεξιᾷ τοῦ θεοῦ καθήμενος.

The next colon (colon 2) is a repetition of the matrix of the preceding colon: τὰ ἄνω φρονεῖτε. It is followed by yet another colon (colon 3) that states the same thing, only negatively: μὴ τὰ ἐπὶ τῆς γῆς (φρονεῖτε). Verse 3 begins with ἀπεθάνετε 'you have died' that cannot be taken literally in this context. So, the καί that follows is not an indication of additional events, but is rather an explanation of what is meant by ἀπεθάνετε. The καί is epexegetic, not copulative. Therefore ἀπεθάνετε . . . θεῷ is one construction, and for that matter one colon (colon 4).

The matrix of the last part of the passage is ὑμεῖς φανερωθήσεσθε which has three stipulations added, namely σὺν αὐτῷ, ἐν δόξῃ and ὅταν . . . ὑμῶν, of which the ending is itself an extension, that is, ἡ ζωὴ ὑμῶν is an extension of Χριστός. All these elements are linked together to form one colon (colon 5) that can be schematized as:

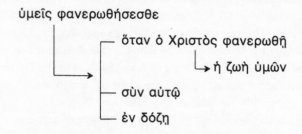

ὑμεῖς φανερωθήσεσθε

ὅταν ὁ Χριστὸς φανερωθῇ

ἡ ζωὴ ὑμῶν

σὺν αὐτῷ

ἐν δόξῃ

The matrix element of colon 1, τὰ ἄνω ζητεῖτε, is repeated in colons 2 and 3, and motivated in colon 4, of which colon 5 gives the result. The close link between colons 4 and 5 is emphasized by the chiastic structure of the elements:

<u>ἀπεθάνετε</u> γάρ , καὶ <u>ἡ ζωὴ ὑμῶν</u> <u>κέκρυπται</u> σὺν
     A1   A2   A3

<u>τῷ Χριστῷ</u> ἐν <u>τῷ θεῷ.</u> ὅταν ὁ <u>Χριστὸς</u>
     A4   B4

<u>φανερωθῇ,</u> <u>ἡ ζωὴ ὑμῶν,</u> τότε καὶ
     B3   B2

<u>ὑμεῖς σὺν αὐτῷ φανερωθήσεσθε ἐν δόξῃ</u>
                    B1

The four aspects that are underlined as A1, A2, A3, and A4 are repeated in an inverse order as B1, B2, B3, and B4. So the correlate of A1 is B1, of A2 is B2, and so on. This chiastic arrangement represents a style which ancient rhetoricians described as σχῆμα διανοίας. The double chiasmus can be represented as:

A1   A4

          A2   A3

          B3   B2

B4   B1

Semantically the chiasmus highlights the following: the revelation in glory with Christ (B1) is opposed to the death to the world (A1). This occurs when one's life (A2) is absorbed into Christ so that he becomes one's life (B2). The consequence of this is suggested in A3 and B3: 'your hiddenness is transformed by Christ's manifestation'. It should be observed that the word Χριστός of A4 and B4, at the end of the first group and at the beginning of the second group, emphasizes Christ as the vital factor with τῷ θεῷ as the link.

Col 3:1–4 is an illustration of how the structure of separate colons contributes to the construction of the colons in relation to each other. It has shown in this passage that colons 4 and 5 form a cluster.

With the above analysis the text of Col 3:1–4 can now be schematized as follows to indicate the relationships between the colons. These relationships represent the line of argument:

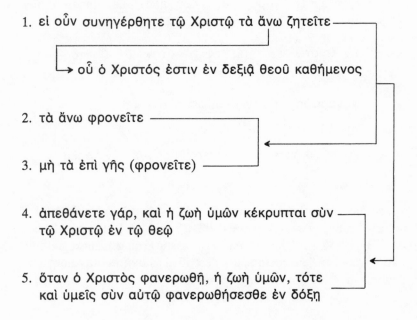

1. εἰ οὖν συνηγέρθητε τῷ Χριστῷ τὰ ἄνω ζητεῖτε

         οὗ ὁ Χριστός ἐστιν ἐν δεξιᾷ θεοῦ καθήμενος

2. τὰ ἄνω φρονεῖτε

3. μὴ τὰ ἐπὶ γῆς (φρονεῖτε)

4. ἀπεθάνετε γάρ, καὶ ἡ ζωὴ ὑμῶν κέκρυπται σὺν τῷ Χριστῷ ἐν τῷ θεῷ

5. ὅταν ὁ Χριστὸς φανερωθῇ, ἡ ζωὴ ὑμῶν, τότε καὶ ὑμεῖς σὺν αὐτῷ φανερωθήσεσθε ἐν δόξῃ

As was said above, the pivot point of the passage is the expression τὰ ἄνω ζητεῖτε/φρονεῖτε which is to follow upon εἰ οὖν συνηγέρθητε τῷ Χριστῷ and motivated in colon 4 of which colon 5 gives the result.

On this basis we may restate the structure of the argument as:

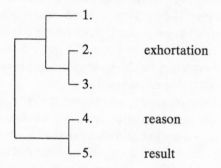

This analyzed section (Col 3:1–4) should be seen over against the preceding section because the previous paragraph (Col 2:20–23) begins with εἰ ἀπεθάνετε τῷ Χριστῷ, which is contrasted in colon 1 above (Col 3:1). This highlights the reason—result given in colons 4 and 5, and so τὰ ἄνω ζητεῖτε/φρονεῖτε is fully motivated as the pivot point of Col 3:1–4. Just as ἀγάπη and πίστις were taken to be the pivot point of the first example (Philem 4–7), so τὰ ἄνω ζητεῖτε/φρονεῖτε appears as the focal element of Col 3:1–4. Part of the justification for a discourse analysis based on colon structure is precisely this fact that the basic thrust of a text can be determined through the use of linguistically motivated methods. This type of discourse analysis aims at unfolding an arrangement or schematization of thought in order to promote a better understanding of the text.

Example 3: 1 Corinthians 12:4–11

In the previous examples the question arose as to how we can tell which part of a complete text can be taken as a paragraph. This problem will now be dealt with by using 1 Cor 12:4–11 as an example. Editions of the NT are usually printed in paragraphs, as in the case of the *UBSGNT* text which was used in the examples so far discussed. This paragraphing of the text was, however, not based on any formal linguistic criteria. As is done in most commentaries, the flow of the contents of the text is followed and this generally forms the basis of the paragraphing of the text. In many cases this is useful because through the ages a large amount of knowledge has been gathered about the NT which has enabled editors to mark out the paragraphs fairly well. Yet this method can hardly be called scientific. Elements such as introductory particles may also be kept in mind in determining the beginning of a paragraph, but even here it is not possible to be free of personal prejudice. Traditional methods need not be completely rejected for they can very often be the starting point, provided that they are not seen as sufficient in themselves.

The marking out of the paragraph rests upon the structure. The dilemma is that we can only find structure after an analysis. For practical reasons it is necessary to begin with the traditional material and after a section has been worked on, the structural relationship between the colons should indicate whether the selected section can still be considered a unity or not. When the pattern or structure of closely related colons has come to an end, the break in the linking between colons will be a sure indication of paragraphing. One of the most common patterns is that of *ring composition*, which is found when the text finishes with the same idea as it started with. When the ring is completed a paragraph is found. This would lead one to analyze 1 Cor 12:1–11 as containing two pericopes although the *UBSGNT* shows it to be one. Verses 4–11 form a typical structure of ring composition, while the first three verses have their own structure in which each proposition leads to the next without returning.

In order to analyze the semantic content of 1 Cor 12:4–11 the first step would be to mark out the colons. Verse 4 contains two colons since τὸ δὲ αὐτὸ πνεῦμα is not a part of the construction of εἰσίν, but represents a new sentence that contrasts with the first part of verse 4. In verse 6, ὁ ἐνεργῶν τὰ πάντα ἐν πᾶσιν is not a third colon since it is only an extension of θεός. So the construction begins with ὁ δὲ αὐτὸς θεός and finishes with ἐν πᾶσιν. Verse 7 is one colon that has a structure analogous to a sentence such as 'he always gives him'. (See the construction of verse 7 at the top of the facing page.)

The sentence 'he always gives him' consists of a subject 'he' which indicates the nominal (N) part of the sentence. The verbal (V) part consists of the event 'give' plus the extension 'always him'. The extension fixes the time of the event and contains the benefited (indirect object). The sentence is one construction since it contains one closely knit structure. The Greek of verse 7 fits structurally into the same pattern, and is therefore one colon. A tree diagram is an adequate test to determine whether a section of the text has more than

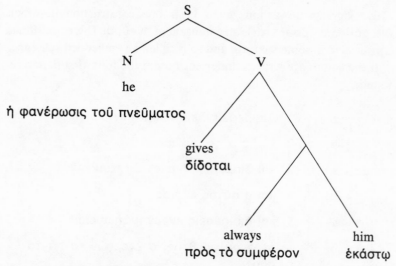

one colon. When all the elements can be attached to one S → N + V, one colon is found. Verse 4, as said, consists of two colons since it has to be analyzed as:

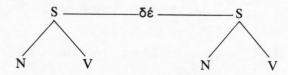

Verses 8 and 9 likewise contain two colons each. Verse 10 has 5 colons, verse 11 has one. Presented as a tree diagram, the structure of verse 11 can be schematized as:

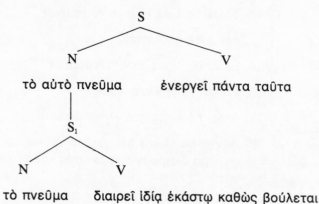

This diagram shows how verse 11 is one construction in which διαιροῦν . . . βούλεται is an extension of πνεῦμα. This extension is constructed in sentence form and so is called an embedded sentence.

If the colons are written under each other the following pattern is found:

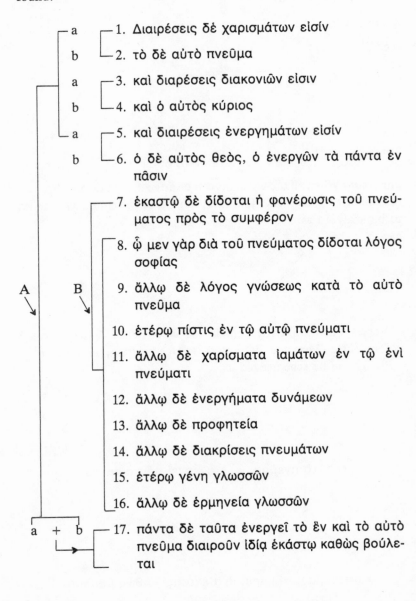

a   1. Διαιρέσεις δὲ χαρισμάτων εἰσίν
b   2. τὸ δὲ αὐτὸ πνεῦμα

a   3. καὶ διαρέσεις διακονιῶν εἰσιν
b   4. καὶ ὁ αὐτὸς κύριος

a   5. καὶ διαιρέσεις ἐνεργημάτων εἰσίν
b   6. ὁ δὲ αὐτὸς θεὸς, ὁ ἐνεργῶν τὰ πάντα ἐν πᾶσιν

7. ἑκάστῳ δὲ δίδοται ἡ φανέρωσις τοῦ πνεύματος πρὸς τὸ συμφέρον

8. ᾧ μὲν γὰρ διὰ τοῦ πνεύματος δίδοται λόγος σοφίας

9. ἄλλῳ δὲ λόγος γνώσεως κατὰ τὸ αὐτὸ πνεῦμα

10. ἑτέρῳ πίστις ἐν τῷ αὐτῷ πνεύματι

11. ἄλλῳ δὲ χαρίσματα ἰαμάτων ἐν τῷ ἑνὶ πνεύματι

12. ἄλλῳ δὲ ἐνεργήματα δυνάμεων

13. ἄλλῳ δὲ προφητεία

14. ἄλλῳ δὲ διακρίσεις πνευμάτων

15. ἑτέρῳ γένη γλωσσῶν

16. ἄλλῳ δὲ ἑρμηνεία γλωσσῶν

A   B

a + b   17. πάντα δὲ ταῦτα ἐνεργεῖ τὸ ἓν καὶ τὸ αὐτὸ πνεῦμα διαιροῦν ἰδίᾳ ἑκάστῳ καθὼς βούλεται

From this structure 1 Cor 12:4–11 appears to consist of two elements: A presents the case, B provides particulars of the case. In A, which consists of colons 1–6 plus 17, a ring composition is found. Colons 1, 3, and 5 present the *many* (= a) in opposition to the *one* (= b) of colons 2, 4, and 6. In colon 17 this is again found in πάντα (= a) and αὐτό (= b). Thus the ring composition provides a structure in which the *one* as opposed to the *many* is emphasized. By stressing this point Paul accentuates the fact that the Corinthians should not absolutize one gift as they had done with the glossolalia (see 1 Corinthians 14). There is a variety of gifts, yet there is one Spirit who distributes all the gifts. The gifts should not be arranged hierarchically for they are all given by the one Spirit. This contention is repeated in B: the one Spirit gives to everyone. Colon 7 presents the broader proposition which serves as a heading for 8–16. In fact, colons 8–16 provide the details for ἑκάστῳ in colon 7 together with an expansion on the opposition of *one* and *many*. This forms the pivot point of the entire paragraph which was motivated by πρὸς τὸ συμφέρον in colon 7. The purpose of the gifts is that people should benefit from them. The benefit rather than the place in a hierarchy is the guiding line.

It can be seen how the pivot point is touched upon in every colon. A continuous change of style in the presentation highlights the concept of *one* and *many*. In colons 1, 3, and 5 three event words are used, χαρισμάτων, διακονιῶν, ἐνεργημάτων connected to three object words πνεῦμα, κύριος, θεός. The first and the last (πνεῦμα and θεός) are the agents of the events with κύριος the affected. Note also the interchange of δέ and καί. Paul exploits this interaction of words and constructions to emphasize the idea of *one* and *many*.

How is the agent/affected determined? This is done through an analysis of the deep structure. In χαρισμάτων we have an event which has πνεῦμα as agent: the Spirit bestows gifts. The same is true of ἐνεργημάτων and θεός: God works. In the case of διακονιῶν this relationship does not apply. The Lord (κύριος) cannot be the agent because it is not the Lord who serves us. Rather, it is we who serve the Lord: there are many ways to serve (i.e., for us to serve), yet there is only one Lord.

Colons 1–6 emphasize the opposition one/many in a way that can be easily observed. At the end of the paragraph this is once more stated in a shorter way since πνεῦμα now acts as a joint subject. In colons 1–6 the three terms θεός, κύριος, πνεῦμα were mentioned separately, but now all three are combined within πνεῦμα who is indeed the actual agent of the giving of spiritual gifts. Note that colon 17 reads 'the Spirit works (ἐνεργεῖ) everything'. This word has already been found in colons 5 and 6 of God working everything. In colon 17 it is further stated that 'the Spirit distributes as he desires'. This has been hinted at in colon 7 in the use of the words δίδοται πρὸς τὸ συμφέρον. In other words, the Spirit determines which are useful and which are not. This decision is according to his desires.

Colons 8–16 in describing the specific gifts also have different patterns of style: chiasmus (8–9), parallelism (10–11), and free pattern (12–16). These changes are basically stylistic, yet they tone in with the overall notion of the opposition one/many. These patterns are clearest when the κόμματα or phrase units are written beneath one another:

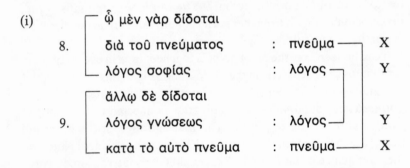

(i) ⌐ ᾧ μὲν γὰρ δίδοται
8. | διὰ τοῦ πνεύματος   : πνεῦμα ——— X
  ⌐ λόγος σοφίας   : λόγος ┐   Y
  | ἄλλῳ δὲ δίδοται
9. | λόγος γνώσεως   : λόγος ┘   Y
  ⌐ κατὰ τὸ αὐτὸ πνεῦμα : πνεῦμα ——— X

Within the chiasmus the word λόγος in λόγος σοφίας and λόγος γνώσεως, contrasts with πνεῦμα and therefore plays a structurally important role, but semantically these expressions are almost lexical units (unitary complexes): λόγος σοφίας = σοφία in a specific situation. The same applies to λόγος γνώσεως. The term λόγος only contributes in keeping the focus on σοφία and γνῶσις as gifts to action in a specific situation, and not merely as general activities. In other words, it does not point to intellectual ability in general, but to the particular gift in a specific situation.

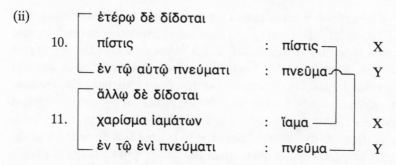

(ii)

10.

ἑτέρῳ δὲ δίδοται

πίστις   : πίστις   X

ἐν τῷ αὐτῷ πνεύματι   : πνεῦμα   Y

11.

ἄλλῳ δὲ δίδοται

χάρισμα ἰαμάτων   : ἴαμα   X

ἐν τῷ ἑνὶ πνεύματι   : πνεῦμα   Y

The fine use of style should be observed. In (i) there is a chiasmus plus an interchange of prepositions with πνεῦμα. In (ii) there is parallelism, but with no interchange of prepositons. In (i) both σοφία and γνῶσις are extended by λόγος, while in (ii) the parallelism is slightly "distorted" by πίστις being in opposition to χάρισμα ἰαμάτων, which is also in the plural. This slight distortion within the parallelism contributes stylistically to avoid overcharacterization. This makes it clear that the interchange of forms, especially prepositions, must not be used in this paragraph to try and determine distinctions of meaning. They do not have any direct semantic function in relation to each other, but only an aesthetic one. Indirectly, however, these interchanges underline the opposition one/many.

(iii)

12.–16.

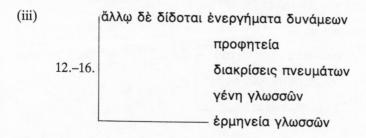

ἄλλῳ δὲ δίδοται ἐνεργήματα δυνάμεων

προφητεία

διακρίσεις πνευμάτων

γένη γλωσσῶν

ἑρμηνεία γλωσσῶν

At first sight there does appear to be some linear pattern in colons 12–16, but actually this is only a free structure that closes the text. In a well-written paragraph we often find loosely structured parts. However, it is still a part of the pattern—in fact, a loose pattern is still a pattern—since it does serve to change the style by reducing its intensity.

Semantics in this paragraph is not restricted to what belongs within the boundary of this paragraph. Semantic considerations reach beyond these bounds. In 1 Cor 12:4–11 colon 7 appeared to be the title of part B with ἑκάστῳ of colon 7 extended in 8–16. The πρὸς τὸ συμφέρον of colon 7 was echoed in colon 17 καθὼς βούλεται, but it also seems to be extended even further since it is repeated in the next paragraph (verses 12–26). This means that ἑκάστῳ is extended in colons 8–16, and πρὸς τὸ συμφέρον (hinted at in colon 17) is extended into the next paragraph. Moreover, when the paragraphs of chapters 12, 13, and 14 are compared they seem to form a unit. Chapters 12 and 14 are closely related to 13, which acts as an explanatory text between them. To determine this, we have to continue our analysis by moving on to 1 Cor 12:12–26.

Example 4: 1 Corinthians 12:12–26
The opening verse of this paragraph consists of a series of interlocking structures in which three constructions are woven together. These constructions are formed into one stretch of language that is embraced by καθάπερ and Χριστός. The final part, οὕτως καὶ ὁ Χριστός, serves as an ending for all three constructions introduced by καθάπερ:

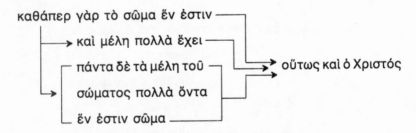

This structure can be rewritten by three colons. Before this is done, the verse which follows, also containing intertwined constructions, must be explained. The grammatical subject πάντες is extended in εἴτε Ἰουδαῖοι εἴτε Ἕλληνες εἴτε δοῦλοι εἴτε ἐλεύθεροι. With πάντες they are all congruent with ἐβαπτίσθημεν. In the same way all three are congruent with ἐποτίσθημεν. Verse 13 consequently has two colons. The remaining part of the paragraph is grammatically less complicated. We can now continue on with the rewriting of the colons.

1. καθάπερ γὰρ τὸ σῶμα ἕν ἐστιν (οὕτως καὶ ὁ Χριστός)
2. (καθάπερ) μέλη πολλὰ ἔχει (οὕτως καὶ ὁ Χριστός)
3. (καθάπερ) πάντα τὰ μέλη τοῦ σώματος πολλὰ ὄντα ἕν ἐστιν σῶμα οὕτως καὶ ὁ Χριστός
4. καὶ γὰρ ἐν ἑνὶ πνεύματι ἡμεῖς πάντες ἐβαπτίσθημεν εἰς ἓν σῶμα εἴτε Ἰουδαῖοι εἴτε Ἕλληνες εἴτε δοῦλοι εἴτε ἐλεύθεροι
5. εἴτε Ἰουδαῖοι εἴτε Ἕλληνες εἴτε δοῦλοι εἴτε ἐλεύθεροι πάντες ἓν πνεῦμα ἐποτίσθημεν
6. καὶ γὰρ τὸ σῶμα οὐκ ἔστιν ἓν μέλος ἀλλὰ πολλά
7. ἐὰν εἴπῃ ὁ πούς, ὅτι οὐκ εἰμὶ χείρ, οὐκ εἰμὶ ἐκ τοῦ σώματος οὐ παρὰ τοῦτο οὐκ ἔστιν ἐκ τοῦ σώματος
8. καὶ ἐὰν εἴπῃ τὸ οὖς ὅτι οὐκ εἰμὶ ὀφθαλμός οὐκ εἰμὶ ἐκ τοῦ σώματος οὐ παρὰ τοῦτο οὐκ ἔστιν ἐκ τοῦ σώματος
9. εἰ ὅλον τὸ σῶμα ὀφθαλμός ποῦ ἡ ἀκοή
10. εἰ ὅλον ἀκοή ποῦ ἡ ὄσφρησις
11. νυνὶ δὲ ὁ θεὸς ἔθετο τὰ μέλη ἓν ἕκαστον αὐτῶν ἐν τῷ σώματι καθὼς ἠθέλησεν
12. εἰ δὲ ἦν τὰ πάντα ἓν μέλος ποῦ υὸ σῶμα
13. νῦν δὲ πολλὰ μὲν μέλη ἓν δὲ σῶμα
14. οὐ δύναται δὲ ὁ ὀφθαλμὸς εἰπεῖν τῇ χειρί, χρείαν σοῦ οὐκ ἔχω
15. ἢ πάλιν ἡ κεφαλὴ τοῖς ποσίν, χρείαν ὑμῶν οὐκ ἔχω
16. ἀλλὰ τὰ δοκοῦντα μέλη τοῦ σώματος ἀσθενέστερα ὑπάρχειν πολλῷ μᾶλλον ἀναγκαῖά ἐστιν
17. καὶ ἃ δοκοῦμεν ἀτιμότερα εἶναι τοῦ σώματος τούτοις τιμὴν περισσοτέραν περιτίθεμεν
18. καὶ τὰ ἀσχήμονα ἡμῶν εὐσχημοσύνην περισσοτέραν ἔχει
19. τὰ δὲ εὐσχήμονα ἡμῶν οὐ χρείαν ἔχει
20. ἀλλὰ ὁ θεὸς συνεκέρασεν τὸ σῶμα τῷ ὑστερουμένῳ περισσοτέραν δοὺς τιμήν ἵνα μὴ ᾖ σχίσμα ἐν τῷ σώματι ἀλλὰ τὸ αὐτὸ ὑπὲρ ἀλλήλων μεριμνῶσιν τὰ μέλη
21. καὶ εἴτε πάσχει ἓν μέλος συμπάσχει πάντα τὰ μέλη
22. εἴτε δοξάζεται ἓν μέλος συγχαίρει πάντα τὰ μέλη

It is striking to see that this paragraph contains two pivot points. This does not usually occur, since two pivot points will involve two paragraphs, but when it does occur as in this passage the two are intertwined. There is such a close relation between them that they are, in fact, two sides of the same coin. In this paragraph the first is found between colons 1 and 13. The theme is "the one in opposition to the many." Actually this is a repetition of the theme of the previous pericope. This thought is so basic that Paul wants to express it time and again in as many forms as possible. In this pericope it is presented in colons 1–3, again in colon 6, and finally in colon 13. The remaining parts between colons 1 and 13 form pairs. Consider the structure:

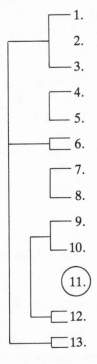

Colon 12 is the exact parallel of colons 9 + 10 but does not follow directly on colons 9 + 10. Colon 12 interrupts this unity, and stands on its own within the structure. In the discussion on the previous paragraph (example 3), it was noted that the words πρὸς τὸ συμφέρον (colon 7 of example 3) were echoed in καθὼς βούλεται (colon 17 of example 3). In the section now examined (example 4), colon 11 is obviously parallel to καθὼς βούλεται, and links with colon 20 to form the second pivot point. In colon 20 πρὸς τό is extended because it accentuates the fact that God gives to every member that which is necessary for each to serve the other without division. Here συμφέρον reappears, and in colons 21 and 22 the thought of colon 20 is again repeated but in a different way. This has the result that the central and all-embracing thought of both paragraphs (examples 3 and 4) can be summarized as follows: God wants all the gifts to work together so as to be of mutual benefit for all the believers.

The fact that example 4 has two pivot points is illustrated by this summary. The themes of both are united or intertwined together due to the fact that colon 11 acts within colons 1–13.

When a paragraph has been analyzed in this way it may give the appearance of being the result of an artificial method. On the surface this may be the case since all the elements are placed next to one another. However, when an author constructs a paragraph he arranges the text so as to reproduce his thoughts in as clear a way as possible. The author has a view of what he wants to say in his mind, and as he unfolds it a repetition of ideas is found to occur. In this way a pattern will naturally appear. In a musical composition this is certainly true, and good literature should not be very different from this. When the works of the Greek rhetoricians are read, for example, Gorgias of Leontini or Demetrius, it is quite clear that they attached great importance to structure.

In returning to example 4, we may now pay more attention to certain aspects of the individual colons, especially the longer ones. The first three colons represent the basic theme of the one/many opposition. Note how this is displayed in the structural arrangement.

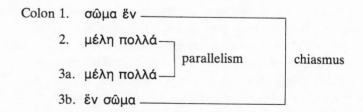

The next group, colons 4 and 5, display the same features:

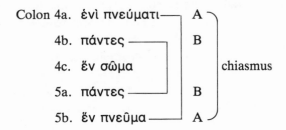

Colon 4a. ἐνὶ πνεύματι — A

4b. πάντες — B

4c. ἕν σῶμα

5a. πάντες — B

5b. ἕν πνεῦμα — A

chiasmus

A chiasmus between certain value judgments is discovered in the series that extends πάντες, namely, εἴτε Ἰουδαῖοι εἴτε Ἕλληνες εἴτε δοῦλοι εἴτε ἐλεύθεροι:

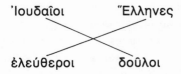

'Ιουδαῖοι   Ἕλληνες

ἐλεύθεροι   δοῦλοι

This chiasmus does not suggest that the Ἰουδαῖοι are ἐλεύθεροι, but that in the series Ἰουδαῖοι—Ἕλληνες the order 'chosen people—heathens' describes a descending scale, while δοῦλοι—ἐλεύθεροι presents an ascending scale.

In colons 7 + 8, 9 + 10, and 12 a parallelism is found and is repeated in 14 + 15. Colons 16–19 have a looser structure which eases the intensity of the style (as in the previous example).

Colons 1–3 are clearly a summary of the contents of the two previous paragraphs. These three colons can therefore just as well serve as an ending to the previous paragraphs. But they also serve as an introduction to the present paragraph. It now also becomes clear how the main line of thought of example 4 was structurally motivated: God gives many things, but in him everything is one. The last part of 1 Corinthians 12 will now be analyzed to enable us to place the three paragraphs in relation to one another.

Example 5: 1 Corinthians 12:27–31

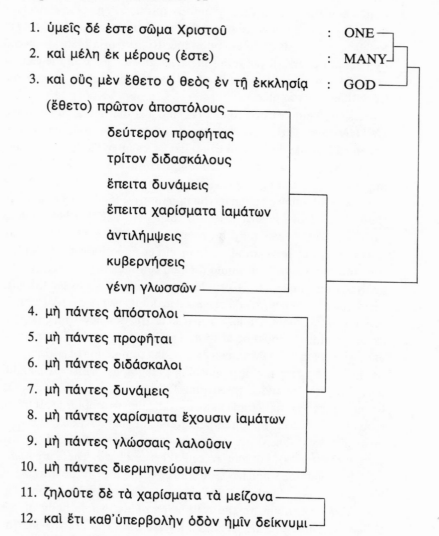

1. ὑμεῖς δέ ἐστε σῶμα Χριστοῦ   : ONE
2. καὶ μέλη ἐκ μέρους (ἐστε)   : MANY
3. καὶ οὓς μὲν ἔθετο ὁ θεὸς ἐν τῇ ἐκκλησίᾳ   : GOD

   (ἔθετο) πρῶτον ἀποστόλους

          δεύτερον προφήτας

          τρίτον διδασκάλους

          ἔπειτα δυνάμεις

          ἔπειτα χαρίσματα ἰαμάτων

          ἀντιλήμψεις

          κυβερνήσεις

          γένη γλωσσῶν

4. μὴ πάντες ἀπόστολοι
5. μὴ πάντες προφῆται
6. μὴ πάντες διδάσκαλοι
7. μὴ πάντες δυνάμεις
8. μὴ πάντες χαρίσματα ἔχουσιν ἰαμάτων
9. μὴ πάντες γλώσσαις λαλοῦσιν
10. μὴ πάντες διερμηνεύουσιν
11. ζηλοῦτε δὲ τὰ χαρίσματα τὰ μείζονα
12. καὶ ἔτι καθ᾽ὑπερβολὴν ὁδὸν ἡμῖν δείκνυμι

A phenomenon typical of discourses is that as soon as a colon is extended, a pattern appears between the elements of the colon. The pattern of colon 3 displays a structure similar to that of colons 4–10. The two patterns state almost the same thing, one positively, the other negatively. However, they do not have an exact "one to one" relationship with each other, but differ slightly so as to accentuate the basic emphasis of Paul's reasoning. By this he attempts to show how one gift cannot be elevated in importance above another. Speaking in tongues, which was of great importance to the Corinthians, is placed by Paul at the end of the series in verses 28 and 30, as in the case of verse 10. Not, on the other hand, to degrade it, but to counter the Corinthian overemphasis.

Verse 31 contains two colons (11 and 12) that are divided in the *UBSGNT* text. The first colon is seen to complete the last paragraph of chapter 12, while the second colon begins chapter 13. This was done due to the influence of the traditional translation of ζηλοῦτε as an imperative. According to this view chapter 12 closes with a list of gifts (colons 3–10) followed by an instruction to strive for the higher gifts. In the outline above colons 1–10 are related to one another. Colons 11–12, however, can only be related if ζηλοῦτε is taken as an imperative, but then colon 11 is in direct opposition to the entire previous argument. Paul would then be contradicting himself. In the analysis of example 3 the Corinthians were urged not to see the gifts hierarchically as they indeed persisted in doing. Every gift is of benefit in contributing to the whole. To give an instruction now with ζηλοῦτε as an imperative would be absurd. The last paragraph of chapter 12 ends with colon 10. As was seen earlier, the completion of a structured group is the norm for distinguishing paragraphs. Verse 31 should, therefore, not be added to chapter 12. The two colons of verse 31 belong to the next paragraph as an introduction to chapter 13. If this is taken to be correct, the three paragraphs of chapter 12 explain how *many* gifts exist. The Corinthians emphasized glossolalia (as is clearly seen in chapter 14), but Paul rejected this emphasis. There are *many* gifts, he maintained, and it is God who gives them all by the working of his Spirit. He does this because all the gifts—not some in particular—contribute to the well-being of the whole body of the believers. Therefore, he can say in verse 31: "you are striving for (ζηλοῦτε as indicative) those gifts you consider to be better or higher, but I want to show you a more excellent way." If you really want to have something within the Christian community you can single out as *the* thing, then make it ἀγάπη, love, which also comes from the Spirit, in fact, it is a "fruit of the Spirit" (Gal 5:22). The next chapter extends this idea. And then in chapter 14 Paul returns to the gifts. The relation of chapters 12–14 of 1 Corinthians can be illustrated as:

| 12 | 13 | 14 |

Example 6: Romans 1:1–7

In most editions of the Greek NT Rom 1:1–7 is printed as one sentence. It begins with Παῦλος which is followed by a series of extensions up to the end of verse 6. Verse 7 begins with a predicate which follows on from an implicit verb of which Παῦλος is the subject: Παῦλος (γράφει) πᾶσιν τοῖς οὖσιν ἐν Ῥώμῃ. The document is a letter, and the style of this passage is typically that of an ancient letter. Therefore the implicit verb in the construction above can be taken to be γράφει. Verse 7b consists of a greeting in the nominative case that begins with χάρις ὑμῖν καὶ εἰρήνη. This is logically a part of the previous statement since Paul extends this greeting, and therefore editions of the Greek NT print it as part of one large sentence. Yet, verse 7b actually forms a different colon, for it is a construction on its own having its own subject, namely θεός and κυρίος.

The extensions from Παῦλος onwards are as follows: First, three extensions of Παῦλος, namely δοῦλος Χριστοῦ Ἰησοῦ, κλητὸς ἀπόστολος, and ἀφωρισμένος εἰς εὐαγγέλιον θεοῦ. The term εὐαγγέλιον is then extended by ὁ προεπηγγείλατο which is itself extended by propositions introduced by διά, ἐν, and περί. The phrase περὶ τοῦ υἱοῦ αὐτοῦ once again has extensions added to υἱοῦ. This pattern continues up to the end of the sentence. Paul's style shows a marked preference for this type of extension known as climactic. Graphically it can be represented as:

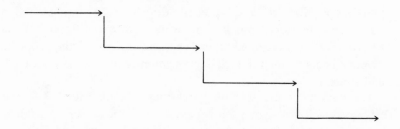

Because χάρις ὑμῖν καὶ εἰρήνη . . . of verse 7b is logically related to what precedes, it can be presented as part of the same paragraph. It is joined more closely to the preceding sentence than to the one following which begins with the πρῶτον of verse 8. Therefore, Rom 1:1—7 is one paragraph with two colons. The first colon is greatly extended and the extensions themselves betray a pattern between their elements. The relationship between the two colons can be illustrated as follows:

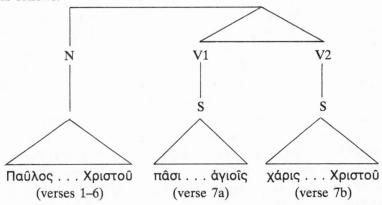

N	V1	V2
Παῦλος . . . Χριστοῦ	πᾶσι . . . ἀγίοις	χάρις . . . Χριστοῦ
(verses 1–6)	(verse 7a)	(verse 7b)

In other words, Paul writes to everyone, and Paul prays that God would give his grace and peace to them. This describes the basic line of thought which Paul wants to convey, namely, that he first wants to present himself and then to send his regards to his readers. In the first part in which he presents himself, the climactic style results in the theme of "Paul and who he is" being quickly abandoned, and exchanged for the theme of "Jesus and who he is." The colon structure of Rom 1:1-7 can now be presented as shown in illustration on facing page.

The arrow connections indicate the relations between the nuclear units of the colon: Παῦλος (γράφει) πᾶσιν has τοῖς οὖσιν ἐν Ῥώμῃ (.2) as an extension defining πᾶσιν while ἀγαπητοῖς θεοῦ (.3) and κλητοῖς ἀγίοις (.4) are additional characterizations of 'the people in Rome'. Then follow three characterizations defining the man Paul, and so on.

The nuclear relations of the extensions 1.5, 1.6, and 1.7 can be explained as follows: In 1.5 it is possession + possessor, in 1.6 it is action + purpose (for κλητός, a so-called passive verbal adjective, is semantically an event word with God as agent and ἀπόστολος as the

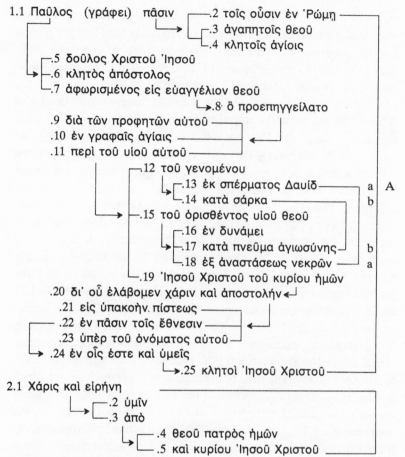

purpose or goal of the event, i.e., 'called to be . . .') and in 1.7 it is again action + purpose (explicitly indicated by the preposition εἰς). These can be restated as:

(a) Paul belongs to Jesus Christ as his servant,

(b) God called Paul to be his messenger,

(c) God separated Paul in order that he may bring God's Good News.

The subject, or agent, of 1.8 (extending εὐαγγέλιον in 1.7) is θεός (already mentioned in 1.7): God promised his Good News long ago. He promised it διά, ἐν, and περί. These three prepositions render the relations as means, location, content. That is to say, God promised this (a) by causing the prophets to speak about it, (b) in the Holy Scriptures, (c) about his Son. In other words, God's Good News was proclaimed long ago by the prophets, preserved in the Holy Scriptures and was concerned with his Son. Or: The Good News which God promised is concerned with his Son. It is found in the Holy Scriptures, and his prophets were the instruments he used to announce it. In 1.1–1.11 there is a progression of ideas moving from Paul to the Good News (the Gospel) to the Son. The remainder of the extensions to the end of the colon (1.25) deal with the Son. The Son is not only dealt with in the larger section of the colon but is also the culminating point of the colon. This shows that Paul is not the focal point of the argument, but the Son is. Paul is merely his bond servant. Even though Paul begins his introduction with his own name, he immediately turns to his relationship to Jesus Christ making Jesus the main feature of the argument. This is achieved by three extensions of υἱός in 1.11. These three involve a description or definition of υἱός referring to his human and divine nature and to his title (1.19) as Jesus our Lord. In 1.12–1.14 his human nature is described: according to the flesh (= human nature) he was born as a descendant of David. Note that the prepositions introducing 1.13 and 1.14 are chiastically repeated in 1.17 and 1.18, contrasting his human and divine nature: as far as his human nature is concerned he was born of David's stock, but as far as his holy being (πνεῦμα ἁγιωσύνης) is concerned his resurrection from death (1.18) showed him powerfully (1.16, that is, without a doubt) to be the Son of God (1.15). The chiastic arrangement is a stylistic device which highlights the semantic content of the statement. The term πνεῦμα means 'personality, inner being, real self' while ἁγιωσύνη refers to the uniqueness of his holy nature. The phrase πνεῦμα ἁγιωσύνης, therefore, means 'his holy being, his real being which is divine'. This is followed by Ἰησοῦ Χριστοῦ τοῦ κυρίου ἡμῶν (1.9), which in itself forms a ring with τοῦ υἱοῦ αὐτοῦ (1.11): the Son is Jesus Christ our Lord. Thus *Jesus* is emphasized as the focal element of the discourse.

In 1.20 the emphasis on Jesus is continued in διά denoting the agent who gave Paul his commission, that is, his privilege to be an apostle. Three prepositional phrases define the nature of Paul's apostleship: εἰς (1.21) signifies the purpose, ἐν (1.22) the location, ὑπέρ (1.23) the benefaction. The ἐν πᾶσιν of 1.22 is taken up again in 1.24 to emphasize that the addressees are especially included in the area of Paul's ministry. And once again (see 1.4) the addressees are defined as people being called to belong to Jesus Christ.

The structure of the discourse clearly shows how *Jesus Christ* is the main theme: in 1.5 Paul is immediately linked to Jesus Christ who is the theme of 1.11–1.23, and to whom the believers in Rome are likewise linked (1.25). The discourse pattern clearly displays the basis of Paul's message and authority, namely, Jesus the risen Lord. Though Rom 1:1–7 is a salutation introducing Paul's letter, it is essentially a statement about Paul's authority.

Example 7: Romans 1:8–17

Many editions of the NT as well as many commentaries take Rom 1:8–15 as a paragraph, with Rom 1:16–17 as a following paragraph. This is based on the judgments that Rom 1:16–17 states the main theme of the letter. A colon analysis shows that Rom 1:14–15 has more formal structural links with Rom 1:16–17 than with Rom 1:8–13. [Determining the length of a paragraph is a decision based on the total structure of a larger stretch of discourse. Therefore, it cannot be properly done until the basic colon analysis is completed. As long as colons or colon clusters link together, one paragraph should be acknowledged. It is only when a clear break in the linking of colons or colon clusters can be determined, that one is justified in acknowledging a new paragraph. In modern writing an author usually indicates paragraphs by indentation or spacing in the printed text, but in ancient writing this was never done. Paragraph division can only be done on semantic considerations based on the total structure of a text. For NT Greek one can readily employ the traditional paragraphing as a starting point. Thus we can take Rom 1:8–15 as a hypothetical paragraph. The first step towards a semantic discourse analysis will now be to mark the colons. Verse divisions in the printed text should not be paid attention to. They merely serve the purposes of reference and have nothing to do with syntactic structuring.]

The first matrix to be observed is εὐχαριστῶ with πρῶτον as an enlargement along with τῷ θεῷ μου, διὰ Ἰησοῦ Χριστοῦ, περὶ πάντων ὑμῶν and ὅτι ἡ πίστις ὑμῶν καταγγέλεται ἐν ὅλῳ τῷ κόσμῳ. These five enlargements may be tabulated under εὐχαριστῶ, or presented as in the textual arrangement, given below, writing πρῶτον on the same line as εὐχαριστῶ. The portraying of the syntactic enlargements is merely a heuristic matter to help the reader see the constituent units at a glance. The reason why πρῶτον is written on the same line as εὐχαριστῶ is because πρῶτον serves as an introductory formula to the whole passage while the other enlargements are specific complements or descriptions having more relevant semantic content than πρῶτον. The colon structure of Rom 1:8–17 can be schematized as:

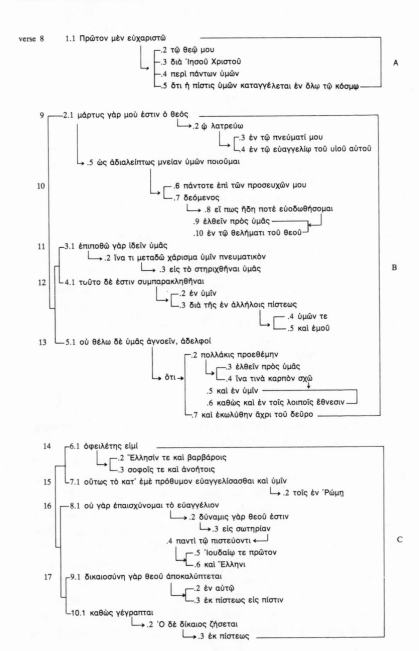

Colon 1 is an expression of thanks introduced by εὐχαριστῶ upon which follows: 1.2 to whom directed, 1.3 the mediator, 1.4 the beneficiary, 1.5 the content. The first three enlargements upon εὐχαριστῶ (1.2, 1.3, 1.4) concern the personages involved, the last (1.5) states the matter or topic, namely their *faith* in Jesus Christ. Throughout the world people are hearing about their faith. This is Paul's reason for expressing his thanks. The theme of colon 1 is an expression of thanks.

The γάρ introducing colon 2 does not add a reason to εὐχαριστῶ or to any other item in colon 1 but applies to the whole. It is therefore a connective, an attention marker adding emphasis to the statement of colon 2. The same applies to the γάρ in colons 3, 8, 9 and the οὕτως in colon 7. Note that the γάρ in 8.2 applies to εὐαγγέλιον, being the δύναμις θεοῦ justifying the statement οὐκ ἐπαισχύνομαι. In 8.2 a feature of εὐαγγέλιον is given and therefore closely linked to 8.1.

Having determined the different colons on the basis of syntactic arguments, the semantic content of each colon should then be taken into account. This involves the content of the enlargements and particularly the relative importance of each enlargement to the whole in order to determine the focal element in the statement. Thus in colon 1 the content of Paul's thanksgiving is the peak of the statement. He is thankful because of their faith. Their faith is the motivation for εὐχαριστῶ, and πίστις is the item continued in the discourse—in fact in section C it builds up to a climax. In colon 2 the string 2.5 is the content of μάρτυς with 2.8 (elaborated in 2.9 and 2.10) being the content of 2.6 and 2.7 (semantically equivalent) which, in turn, give the circumstances of 2.5. The other items in colon 2 linked to θεός are stylistic embellishments, typical of Paul's associative style. The main semantic line runs through the additions to μάρτυς. Therefore, as was said, the content of 2.1 is stated in 2.5: 'God knows that I always pray to be able to visit you'.

The basic semantic content of colons 1 and 2 can now be formulated as:

1. giving thanks for their faith
2. wanting to visit them.

Colon 3 gives the purpose for his longing to visit them, namely to share spiritual blessings. Colon 4 elaborates on this statement of purpose. Therefore colons 3 and 4 can be combined. They have a closer semantic relationship to each other than to either colons 2 or 5.

Colon 5 repeats the content of colons 3 and 4 with the addition of a statement to the effect that his planning to see them did not as yet become effective (5.7). Colon 5 stands in a closer relationship to colons 3 and 4 than to colon 2, since 5 is a summary statement of colons 3 and 4. Therefore colons 3, 4, and 5 are elaborations on colon 2 as indicated by the diagonal lines (in the outline above) linking colons 2–5. Colons 3–5 add to colon 2 forming one cluster with colon 2. That is to say: colon 2 states Paul's longing to see them, while colons 3, 4, and 5 specify the content and purpose of his longing to see them. It is to share in what God gives by means of his Spirit in order (3.3) to be strengthened. The context shows that the reference is to spiritual (not physical) strength, as is explained in colon 4 referring to a strengthening which comes through their mutual faith. The flow of the argument can be restated as: 'I very much want to come and see you so that our mutual faith might help us as we share in the good things that God gives by means of his Spirit'. On the basis of the relationships between the items of thought expressed in colons 2–5, the theme of section B (constituted by colon cluster 2–5) can be summarized as: 'I want to come and see you to share our faith'.

Colon 6 starts a new statement; 6.2 and 6.3 are semantically similar (implying all mankind), being a complement to ὀφειλέτης εἰμί. Colon 6 states Paul's obligation to mankind. The term οὕτως introducing colon 7 states a result following colon 6, the total sum of which implies that Paul must preach the gospel to all people. Colon 7, therefore, continues the statement by showing that the believers in Rome naturally are part of mankind, and that Paul's obligation concerns the bringing of the gospel. The term εὐαγγελίσασθαι is taken up in colon 8, which is a motivation for colons 6–7. Therefore verse 16 of Romans 1 links closely to verse 15 (colon 7). In colons 8, 9, and 10 the nature of the gospel is specified: the gospel is God's powerful method to save the believer (colon 8). Colon 8 defines εὐαγγέλιον (8.2) along with its effect (8.3) and its range of applicability (8.4). Item 8.4 is specified in 8.5 and 8.6. Colon 9 justifies the statement made in colon 8, focusing on 8.1 by 9.2, and on 8.4 by 9.3. Colon 9, therefore, motivates colon 8: it is *faith* from beginning to end (9.3) by which God puts man right with himself. Colon 10 gives authoritative sanction to the statement made in colon 9, namely, Scriptural proof: 'he who is put right with God through faith shall live'.

This shows that colons 6–10 form a cluster, with πίστις as the peak of the argument. The whole paragraph (Rom 1:8–17) builds up towards the final statement ὁ δὲ δίκαιος ἐκ πίστεως ζήσεται. The line of argument in Rom 1:8–17 can now be summarized as:

(A) giving thanks for their faith

(B) wanting to visit them to share their mutual faith

(C) This (=B) entails the gospel which is based on faith.

Faith is the link between sections (A), (B), and (C). It is the pivot point of the paragraph which, along with paragraph 1, forms the introduction to Paul's letter to the believers in Rome.

The exposition given above has shown that one of the most important features of semantic discourse analysis is the proper notation of the case relationships between items, such as content, result, purpose, source, range, and so on. It is these relationships which contribute to a large extent to the semantic information deduced from the colons and to determining the main line of thought.

Example 8: Romans 2:1–16

In the previous section (Rom 1:18–32) Paul has shown how corrupt man is. He now turns to his reader (or audience): "Do you find it shocking to hear about man's depravity? Don't judge mankind to be wicked without looking at yourself, you ὦ ἄνθρωπε πᾶς ὁ κρίνων. You have no excuse, for you are guilty of the same."

At first it appears as if a break exists between ὁ κρίνων and ἐν ᾧ in colon 1. If so, colon 1 would have to be analyzed as two colons. A tree diagram, illustrating the syntactic structure, shows that there is only one construction, and thus one colon. The construction divides the verbal part into a verb-group (vg) and an adverbial group (adv-g), the latter consisting of two embedded sentences. So we have:

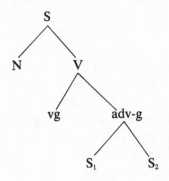

or more fully

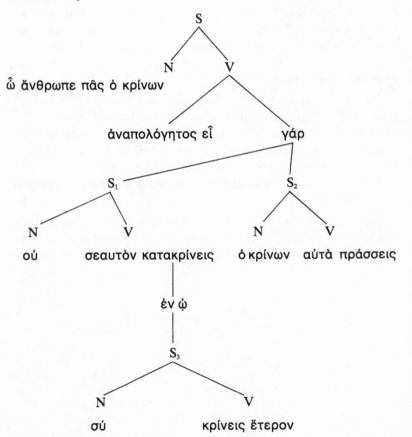

The arrangement of the colons is:

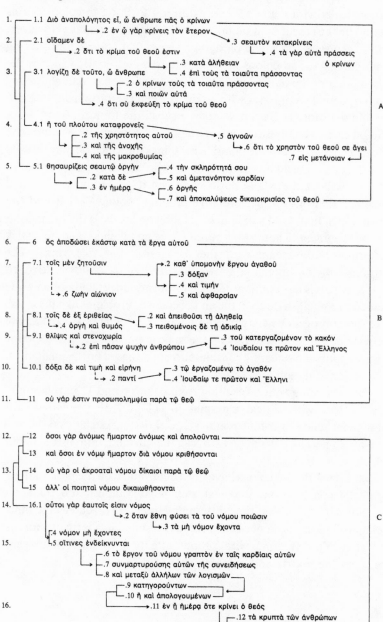

The part marked out as colon 6 in this outline may be taken syntactically with colon 5 as an extension to θεός in colon 5. This would be the case if ὅς is taken as a mere relative pronoun. However, the structure of the whole paragraph shows that colon 6 forms a ring with colon 11, and colons 6–11 constitute a cluster (B) which is the pivot point of the paragraph. This shows that colon 6, though linking with 5, actually contrasts with colon 11. The ὅς introducing colon 6 should therefore rather be taken as a substitute for καὶ οὗτος, since the ὅς carries emphasis. It is not a relative pronoun but a connective particle. This is one of the possible meanings for which ὅς may be used in NT Greek. Deciding whether ὅς = 'who' or 'and he' is a matter of the analysis of the whole pericope. Even if, at the outset, we had assumed that ὅς is a mere relative pronoun, colons 7–11 would still have shown that 'God's judgment is based on deeds' is the pivot point of the argument. Therefore it is not ὅς being taken as 'and he' which determines the meaning of the paragraph, but vice versa. The structure of the argument shows that ἀποδώσει ἑκάστῳ κατὰ τὰ ἔργα αὐτοῦ is a prominent feature of the argument and not an aside added to embellish θεοῦ at the end of colon 5. Problems like these will occasionally occur when two meanings of a particular term can be both applied to the context purely on syntactic arguments. Which meaning really applies is a semantic consideration to be based on the meaning of the total paragraph.

The ring composition resulting from colons 6 and 11 in relation to each other, with a neat chiasmus in colons 7–10 (explaining the statement made in colons 6 and 11), clearly marks colons 6–11 as a cluster. Therefore Rom 2:1–16 can be divided into three major clusters: A, B, C.

Once the different colons have been determined on the basis of their syntactic construction, the next step is to establish the semantic relationship between the different colons. To determine this relationship, the content of each colon is restated in a form as short as possible. This is done with proper attention to the relationship between the matrix and enlargements of each colon.

1. you have no excuse because you who judge others are
   guilty of the same

2. God will judge people who do like you

3. do you think you will escape God's judgment   A

4. don't despise God's kindness wanting you to repent

5. your attitude will bring greater punishment upon you

6. God will judge deeds

7. to those doing good he will do good things

8. to those doing bad he will do bad things

9. bad things will be done to those doing bad   B

10. good things will be done for those doing good

11. God has no prejudice

12. Gentiles sin and are lost apart from the Law

13. Jews having the Law will be judged by it

14. hearing the Law is not enough   C

15. doing the Law is required

16. Gentiles obeying the Law show that the Law
    is in their hearts

According to our theory, the different colons represent the statement units. For Rom 2:1–16 we have sixteen colons of which some have the same semantic content or are contrastive with respect to each other. The next step is to define these contrasts and similarities. Colons 7 and 10 are semantically the same, as are colons 8 and 9, but colons 7 and 10 contrast with colons 8 and 9. They are preceded by colon 6 and followed by colon 11 expressing the same idea, namely, that God has no favorites: only a person's deeds will count before him. These can now be represented as:

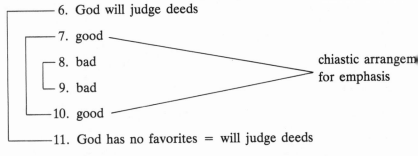

6. God will judge deeds
7. good
8. bad
9. bad
10. good
11. God has no favorites = will judge deeds

chiastic arrangem[ent]
for emphasis

The section (colons 1-5) preceding this clearly contrastive set (colons 6–11) deals mainly with God's judgment which is, in fact, spelled out in colons 6–11. Colons 2 and 5 are more or less similar in content: what you are doing will evoke judgment. Colons 3 and 4 contrast (positive/negative) with respect to God's punishment: God will punish (= you will not escape), yet God wants to pardon. These four colons constitute a chiasmus (punishment + not escape : will escape [be pardoned] + punishment) emphasizing God's judgment. As such it elaborates on colon 1. Therefore the first 5 colons can be related as:

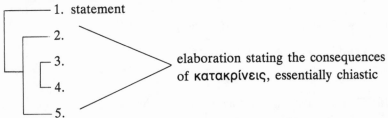

1. statement
2.
3.
4.
5.

elaboration stating the consequences of κατακρίνεις, essentially chiastic

Colons 1–5 constitute cluster A, colons 6–11 cluster B, while colons 12–16 give us cluster C. Colons 12–16 relate to each other as follows: colons 12 and 13 contrast Jew and Gentile. Colons 14 and 15 contrast hearers and doers of the Law. Colon 16 summarizes the implications: the Gentiles are doers, therefore (by implication) the Jews having the Law must be careful not to be hearers only. Cluster C amplifies B: it is deeds that count—doing the Law, not just hearing it, is the point.

The above shows that cluster A is spelled out in B, while C amplifies B. Cluster B is the pivot point of the paragraph. The main argument of Rom 2:1–16 can now be formulated as: *God's judgment is righteous—man will be judged according to his deeds!*

The chiasmus in cluster B can be analyzed even further to indicate finer points of structure. Colon 7, for that matter, has as matrix τοῖς ζητοῦσιν ἀποδώσει. Though τοῖς ζητοῦσιν elaborates on ἑκάστῳ in colon 6, it should not be embedded along with ἑκάστῳ, since the chiastic arrangement of the items in colons 7–10 gives it sufficient emphasis to interpret the construction as elliptic. There ἀποδώσει should be supplied with τοῖς ζητοῦσιν. The same applies logically to colons 8, 9, and 10, although in colons 8, 9, and 10 a switch in syntactic construction results in the complements with ἀποδώσει now being the subjects of the construction. This switch in construction also points to the fact that τοῖς ζητοῦσιν in colon 7 should be understood as a statement on its own, and therefore not embedded with ἑκάστῳ in colon 6. Therefore colon 7 can be analyzed as:

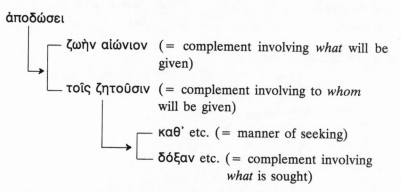

ἀποδώσει

ζωὴν αἰώνιον (= complement involving *what* will be given)

τοῖς ζητοῦσιν (= complement involving to *whom* will be given)

καθ' etc. (= manner of seeking)

δόξαν etc. (= complement involving *what* is sought)

Note that in the structural outline ζωὴν αἰώνιον (7.6) is linked to τοῖς by a broken line indicating that a verbal element (ἀποδώσει) is to be supplied.

Colon 7 can now be restated as: God will give a reward (= eternal life) to those seeking glory, honor, immortal life (= their deeds) by keeping on to do what is good (= their manner of behavior involving an attitude, namely persistence).

Colon 7, therefore, has three basic semantic features: reward, deed, attitude.

In colon 8 the phrases 8.1–3 occupy the same syntactic position as 7.1–5 in colon 7, that is, they give the complement stating *to whom* will be given, while 8.4 states *what* will be given. 8.4 is the reward, 8.2 and 8.3 give the deed (stated negatively and positively) while ἐξ ἐριθείας in 8.1 specifies the attitude. Colons 7 and 8 comprise the first half of the chiasmus announcing what will happen at God's judgment to those doing good (colon 7) and those doing bad (colon 8). In each case the reward for a deed done, with a particular attitude accompanying the deed, is explicitly stated.

Colons 9 and 10 give the second half of the chiasmus. Note that the switch in construction goes even further than in colon 8, for in colon 8 a passive ellipse of ἀποδώσει (to be supplied from colon 6) may be added to complete the construction (therefore the broken line linking τοῖς in 8.1 with 8.4), while in colon 9 some "synonym" such as 'will come upon' should be supplied to link 9.1 with 9.2. In colon 10, however, a passive ellipse of ἀποδώσει can again be assumed. These variations in construction serve to embellish the style while they also add to the contrastive features of the chiastic arrangement of statement units by emphasizing the dichotomy.

Colon 9 can be analyzed as:

```
┌─ 9.1   reward
│
│  9.2   person(s) affected ─┐
│                            │
└─ 9.3   deed                │
                             │
   9.4   person(s) affected ─┘
```

The same applies to colon 10, which indicates that the second half of the chiasmus also shows a repetition of items as in the first half of the chiasmus: the reward and deed of all people (whether bad [colon 9] or good [colon 10]) are set in a resultant relationship to each other, that is, the reward will result from the deed. In other words: deeds determine the reward—and this applies to everybody, a fact emphasized by 9.2 and 10.2, repeated in 9.4 and 10.4. In both 9.4 and 10.4 the word order τε πρῶτον καί should be noted. Regularly when πρῶτον designates a preference or advancement, the word order would be πρῶτον τε καί:

first the one, and then the other. The meaning would then be that the matter actually applies to the first item, but that the second one can also be added. The order in 9.4 and 10.4 softens this contrast, suggesting that what applies to the first item also applies to the latter. This means that though πρῶτον τε καί does not deny a certain priority (referring to God's revelation to mankind), the chronological aspect is not in focus. Therefore 9.4 and 10.4 may be interpreted as 'this applies to Jews and to Gentiles alike'—a fact already mentioned in 9.2 in the rather elaborate phrase ἐπὶ πᾶσαν ψυχὴν ἀνθρώπου, repeated by way of reduction in παντί (10.2).

The internal parts of colons 7–10, often called commata (after the term κόμμα in Demetrius περὶ ἑρμενείας) relate to each other in the following outline of the discussion above:

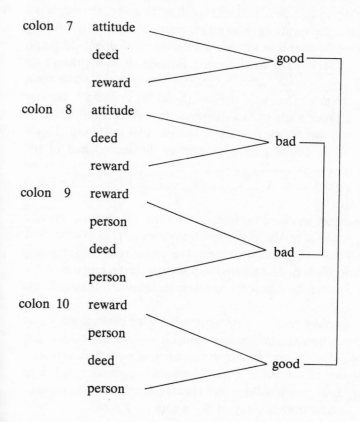

Note also that in colon 8 the double formulation of the *deed* (8.2 and 8.3) shows a chiastic pattern with regard to the positive/negative features of the items:

ἀπειθοῦσι τῇ ἀληθείᾳ

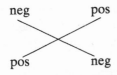

πειθομένοις τῇ ἀδικίᾳ

Another feature of emphasis is the item *reward* which occurs in all four parts of the chiasmus: in the first half at the end of the list; in the second half at the beginning. This arrangement contributes stylistically to the focus of cluster B in which *reward,* along with *deed* (which also occurs in all four parts of the chiasmus), forms the basis of colons 7–10 which are enlargements upon ἀποδώσει (reward) and κατὰ ἔργα (deed) in colon 6. The item 'person' (ἑκάστῳ) in colon 6 likewise occurs in all four parts of the chiasmus, though in the first half it functions in a way supplementary to the attitudes expressed. This is balanced by its doubling in each part of the second half of the chiasmus. Colon 11 echoes colon 6, completing a neatly structured cluster, the pivot point of the argument: *man will be judged according to his deeds.*

The examples analyzed present some of the different aspects of a discourse analysis, yet the most important semantic principle that they illustrate is that every separate element receives "real" meaning only within the whole text. This means that the entire text is instrumental in choosing between the different possible meanings of the sentences and words.

When the pivot point of a paragraph has been determined it may then be seen how the author has built his sentences, phrases, and words around it. In determining the meaning of units such as words, one must not follow the popular traditional approach which uses etymology and a restricted sentence context, but rather the meanings must be derived from a study of the whole paragraph.

Bibliography

Abraham, S. and A. Kiefer
    1966   *A Theory of Structural Semantics.* The Hague: Mouton.

Barclay, William
    1975   *New Testament Words.* The Daily Study Bible. Philadelphia: Westminster Press.

Barr, James
    1961   *Semantics of Biblical Language.* Oxford: Oxford University Press.

Barrett, Charles Kingsley
    1967   *Jesus and the Gospel Tradition.* Philadelphia: Fortress Press.
    1968   *A Commentary on the First Epistle to the Corinthians.* Harper's New Testament Commentaries. New York: Harper and Row.
    1978   *The Gospel According to St. John,* 2d ed. Philadelphia: Westminster Press.

Bloomfield, Leonard
    1933   *Language.* London: Allen and Unwin.

Boman, Thorleif
    1954   *Das hebräische Denken im Vergleich mit dem Griechischen.* Göttingen: Vandenhoeck and Ruprecht.

Bréal, Michel
    1897   *Essai de Semantique.* Paris: Hachette.

Brown, R.
    1958   *Words and Things.* Toronto: Free Press.

Brown, T. H.
    1968   "Good News for Modern Man—Today's English Version," *Biblical Witness* 19.

Carnap, Rudolf
    1964   "Foundations of Logic and Mathematics," in Jerry A. Fodor and Jerrold J. Katz, eds., *The Structure of Language.* Englewood Cliffs: Prentice-Hall, Inc.

Chafe, Wallace L.
    1970   *Meaning and the Structure of Language.* Chicago: University of Chicago Press.
    1971   "Directionality and Paraphrase," *Language* 47: 1–26.
    1972   "Discourse Structure and Human Knowledge," in John B.

Carroll and Roy O. Freedle, eds., *Language Comprehension and the Acquisition of Knowledge.* Washington, D.C.: V. H. Winston.

1973   "Language and Memory," *Language* 49: 261-281.

Chomsky, Noam

1957   *Syntactic Structures.* Janua Linguarum Series Minor 4. The Hague: Mouton.

1965   *Aspects of the Theory of Syntax.* Cambridge, Mass.: The M.I.T. Press.

1966a   "Topics in the Theory of Generative Grammar," in Thomas A. Sebeok, ed., *Theoretical Foundations.* Current Trends in Linguistics 3. The Hague: Mouton.

1966b   *Cartesian Linguistics.* New York: Harper and Row.

1972   Studies on Semantics in Generative Grammar. The Hague: Mouton.

Clark, D. J.

1976   "Some Problems of Being Natural and Producing the Right Meaning," *The Biblical Translator* 27: 213–215.

Conklin, Harold C.

1967   "Lexicographical Treatment of Folk Taxonomies," in Fred W. Householder and Sol Saporta, eds., *Problems in Lexicography.* The Hague: Mouton.

Coseriu, E. and H. Geckeler

1974   "Linguistics and Semantics," in Thomas A. Sebeok, ed., *Linguistics and Adjacent Arts and Sciences.* Current Trends in Linguistics 12. The Hague: Mouton.

Cremer, J. A., ed.

1967   *Catenae Graecorum Patrum in Novum Testamentum,* Vol. 2. Olms: Hildesheim.

Daube, D.

1950   "Jesus and the Samaritan Woman: The Meaning of συγχράο-μαι," *Journal of Biblical Literature* 69: 137–147.

Deibler, E. W.

1968   "Translating for Basic Structure," *The Biblical Translator* 19: 14–16.

Dinneen, Francis P.

1967   *An Introduction to General Linguistics.* New York: Holt, Rinehart and Winston.

Evans, Gareth and John McDowell

1976   *Truth and Meaning: Essays in Semantics.* Oxford: Clarendon Press.

Fodor, Jerry A. and Jerrold J. Katz, eds.

1964   *The Structure of Language.* Englewood Cliffs: Prentice-Hall, Inc.

Fodor, Janet Dean

1977   *Semantics: Theories of Meaning in Generative Grammar.* New York: Crowell.

Friedrich, G.
1959   "Die Problematik eines Teologischen Wörterbuchs zum neuen
               Testament," in Kurt Aland, ed., *Studia Evangelica*. Berlin:
               Akademie-Verlag.

Fries, Charles C.
1954   "Meaning and Linguistic Analysis," *Language* 30: 57–68.

Goppelt, L.
1972   *Theological Dictionary of the New Testament*, Vol. 8. G.
               Friedrich, ed. Grand Rapids, Mich.: Eerdmans.

Grimes, Joseph E. and Naomi Glock
1970   "A Saramaccan Narrative Pattern," *Language* 46: 408–425.

Hall, D. R.
1971   "The Meaning of συγχράομαι in John 4:9," *The Expository
               Times* 83:56–57.

Hendriksen, W.
1953–4   *Exposition of the Gospel According to John*. 2 vols. Grand
               Rapids, Mich.: Baker Book House.

Herbert, A. G.
1955   "Faithfulness and Faith," *Theology* 58: 373–379.

Herder, Johann Gottfried von
1833   *The Spirit of Hebrew Poetry*. James Marsh, tr. Burlington: E.
               Smith.

Hofmann, J. B.
1950   *Etymologisches Wörterbuch des Griechischen*. Munich: Olden-
               bourg.

Hofmann, T. Ron
1976   "Varieties of Meaning," *Language Sciences* 39:6–18.

Hoijer, Harry
1953   "The Relation of Language to Culture," in A. L. Kroeber, ed.,
               Anthropology Today. Chicago: University of Chicago Press.

Hutchins, W. J.
1971   "Semantics in Three Formal Models of Language," *Lingua* 28:
               201–236.

Jakobson, Roman O.
1959   "On Linguistic Aspects of Translation," in R. A. Brown, ed., *On
               Translation*. Cambridge, Mass.: Harvard University Press.

Jordan, J. E.
1965   *Using Rhetoric*. New York: Harper and Row.

Kasher, A.
1972   "Sentences and Utterances Reconsidered," *Foundations of
               Language* 8: 313–345.

Katz, Jerrold J.
1964   "Semi-Sentences," in Jerry A. Fodor and Jerrold J. Katz, eds.,
               The Structure of Language. Englewood Cliffs: Prentice-Hall, Inc.
1965   *The Philosophy of Language*. New York: Harper and Row.

Katz, Jerrold J. and Jerry A. Fodor
    1963   "The Structure of a Semantic Theory," *Language* 39: 170–210.

Knight, George A. F.
    1953   *A Biblical Approach to the Doctrine of the Trinity.* Edinburgh: Oliver and Boyd.

Kodell, Jerome
    1974   "The Word of God Grew," *Biblica* 55: 505–519.

Mauro, Tullio de
    1967   *Ludwig Wittgenstein—His Place in the Development of Semantics.* Dordrecht: D. Reidel.

McCawley, James D.
    1968   "The Role of Semantics in a Grammar," in Emmon Bach and Robert T. Harms, eds., *Universals in Linguistic Theory.* New York: Holt, Rinehart and Winston.

Moravcsik, J. M. E.
    1974   "Linguistics and Philosophy," in Thomas A. Sebeok, ed., *Linguistics and Adjacent Arts and Sciences.* Current Trends in Linguistics 12. The Hague: Mouton.

Morris, Leon
    1958   *The First Epistle of Paul to the Corinthians: An Introduction and Commentary.* The Tyndale New Testament Commentaries. Grand Rapids, Mich.: Eerdmans.

Nida, Eugene A.
    1954   *Customs and Cultures.* New York: Harper.
    1964   *Towards a Science of Translating.* Leiden: Brill.
    1972   "Communication and Translation," *The Bible Translator* 23: 309–316.
    1975a   *Exploring Semantic Structures.* Munich: Fink.
    1975b   "Semantic Structure and Translating," *The Bible Translator* 26: 120–132.
    1975c   *Componential Analysis of Meaning.* The Hague: Mouton.
    1975d   "Language and Psychology," *The Bible Translator* 26: 308–313.
    1979   "Translating Means Communicating," *The Bible Translator* 30: 101–107.

Nida, Eugene A. and C. R. Taber
    1969   *The Theory and Practice of Translation.* Leiden: Brill.

Nyíri, J. C.
    1971   "No Place for Semantics," *Foundations of Language* 7: 56–69.

Ogden, C. K. and I. A. Richards
    1923   *The Meaning of Meaning.* London: Routledge.

Oller, John W., Jr.
    1972   "On the Relation between Syntax, Semantics and Pragmatics," *Linguistics* 83: 43–55.

Padučeva, E. V.
    1972   "On the Structure of the Paragraph," *Linguistics* 131: 49–58.

Pei, Mario
1966   *Glossary of Linguistic Terminology.* New York: Columbia University Press.

Pop, F. J.
1964   *Bijbelse woorden en hun Geheim.* The Hague: Boekencentrum.

Postal, Paul M.
1964   "Underlying and Superficial Linguistic Structures," *Harvard Educational Review* 34: 246–266.

Rabin, Chaim
1958   "The Linguistics of Translation," in A. D. Booth, *Aspects of Translation.* London: Secker and Warburg.

Reichling, Anton
1966a   *Het Taalwetenschap.* Johannesburg: S.A.U.K.
1966b   *Verzamelde Studies over Hedendaagse Problemen der Taalwetenschap.* Zwolle: Willink.

Robertson, A. T.
1931, 1951   *Word Pictures in the New Testament.* Nashville: Broadman.

Robinson, John A. T.
1952   *The Body: A Study in Pauline Theology.* London: SCM Press.

Russell, Bertrand
1940   *An Inquiry into Meaning and Truth.* London: Allen and Unwin.

Sapir, Edward
1907   "Herder's *Ursprung der Sprache,*" *Modern Philology* 5: 109–142.

Saumjan, S. K.
1970   "Semantics and the Theory of Generative Grammars," in A. J. Greimas, ed., *Sign, Language, Culture.* Janua Linguarum Series Maior 1. The Hague: Mouton.

Schwyzer, Eduard
1939   *Griechische Grammatik.* Vol. 1. Munich: C.H. Beck.
1950   Vol. 2. Ed. A. Debrunner.

Siertsema, B.
1969   "Language and World View," *The Bible Translator* 20: 3–21.

Sörensen, H. S.
1970   "Meaning and Reference," in A. J. Greimas, ed., *Sign, Language, Culture.* Janua Linguarum Series Maior 1. The Hague: Mouton.

Stein, P. C.
1974   "On the Restructuring of Discourse," *The Bible Translator* 25: 101–106.

Steinberg, Danny D.
1971   "Overview, Psychology," in Danny D. Steinberg and Leon A. Jakobovits, eds., *Semantics: An Interdisciplinary Reader in Philosophy, Linguistics and Psychology.* Cambridge: Cambridge University Press.
1975   "Semantics from a Psychological Viewpoint," *Language Science* 37: 1–9.

Steinberg, Danny D. and Leon A. Jakobovits, eds.
    1971   *Semantics: An Interdisciplinary Reader in Philosophy, Linguistics and Psychology.* Cambridge: Cambridge University Press.

Torrance, T. F.
    1956/7   "One Aspect of the Biblical Conception of Faith," *Expository Times* 68: 111–114.

Trench, R. C.
    1854   *Synonyms of the New Testament.* Grand Rapids, Mich.: Eerdmans.

Tyler, S. A.
    1969   *Cognitive Anthropology.* New York: Holt, Rinehart and Winston.

Ullman, Stephen
    1962   *Semantics.* New York: Barnes and Noble.

Vincent, M. R.
    1887   *Word Studies in the New Testament.* Reprint 1965. Grand Rapids, Mich.: Eerdmans.

Weinreich, Uriel
    1968   "On the Semantic Structure of Language," in Joseph H. Greenberg, ed., *Universals of Language.* Cambridge, Mass.: The M.I.T. Press.

Wells, Rulon
    1947   "Immediate Constituents," *Language* 23: 81–117.
    1954   "Meaning and Use," *Word* 10: 235–250. Reprint 1961 in Sol Saporta and Jarvis R. Bastian, eds., *Psycholinguistics.* New York: Holt, Rinehart and Winston.

Whorf, Benjamin Lee
    1941   "The Relation of Habitual Thought and Behavior to Language," in Leslie Spier, ed., *Language, Culture and Personality.* Menasha, Wis.: Banta.
    1956   *Language, Thought and Reality.* Cambridge, Mass: The M.I.T. Press.

Wittgenstein, Ludwig
    1953   *Philosophical Investigations.* Oxford: Blackwell.

Wittig, S.
    1977   "A Theory of Multiple Meanings," *Semeia* 9: 75–101.

Wonderly, William L.
    1968   *Bible Translations for Popular Use.* London: United Bible Societies.

Ziff, Paul
    1964   "On Understanding 'Understanding Utterances'," in Jerry A. Fodor and Jerrold J. Katz, eds., *The Structure of Language.* Englewood Cliffs: Prentice-Hall, Inc.

Index of Authors

DATE DUE